# MORMONISM
## A CHRISTIAN RESPONSE

## JOHN R. CONLON

Beacon Hill Press of Kansas City
Kansas City, Missouri

Copyright 2002
by Beacon Hill Press of Kansas City

ISBN: 083-411-9293

Printed in the United States of America

Cover Design: Paul Franitza

**Library of Congress Cataloging-in-Publication Data**

Conlon, John R., 1936-
  Mormonism : a Christian response / John R. Conlon.
    p. cm.
Includes bibliographical referenes.
  ISBN 0-8341-1929-3 (pbk.)
  1. Missions to Mormons. 2. Church of Jesus Christ of Latter-day Saints—Controversial literature. I. Title.
BV2627 .C66 2002
289.3—dc21

                                                    2002014936

10  9  8  7  6  5  4  3  2  1

# CONTENTS

# INTRODUCTION

MEMBERS OF THE CHURCH OF JESUS CHRIST OF LATTER-DAY SAINTS (LDS) are commonly called Mormons. They derive their name from the angel Moroni, who allegedly came to 14-year-old Joseph Smith in 1823 with directions to find the golden plates upon which the records that became the *Book of Mormon* were engraved. But Mormonism was not born until April 6, 1830, following the publication of the *Book of Mormon*.

On the date the church was organized at Palmyra, New York, there were only a handful of followers. In 1831, less than 1,000 faithful followers moved from New York to Kirtland, Ohio. Persecution followed them as they attempted to settle in Missouri and Illinois. In 1844, Smith was incarcerated in the Carthage, Illinois, jail. Later that year, on June 27, he was mortally wounded during a gun battle as a mob stormed the jail.

But their ranks grew rapidly,* and under the able leadership of Brigham Young an estimated 30,000 Mormons trekked across the plains to their Deseret¹ sanctuary in the Salt Lake Valley of Utah in 1846. That represents a portentous growth in only 16 years.

Following a century of relative isolation in their Utah mountain village, LDS membership grew to exceed 1 million by 1947. In the next 55 years membership swelled to its pres-

---

*LDS Mormons are not the only Mormons. Upon the death of Joseph Smith fractures began to surface and the unity of Mormonism was forever splintered. Today there are approximately 17 identifiable groups whose roots go back to the original church founded by Joseph Smith. The largest being the Utah based Church of Jesus Christ of Latter-day Saints. For all practical purposes that is the group we are focusing upon in this book. For a brief description of some of the other groups, see Appendix 2.

ent height of more than 11 million. That is an average growth rate of some 15,000 members a month. With more than 26,000 congregations in 160 countries around the world, Mormonism has come of age. It is estimated that by the year 2080 LDS membership will grow to some 260 million followers,[2] catapulting Mormonism into the ranks of a world religion.

The phenomenal impact of Mormonism's growth reaches into every facet of society. The church already boasts a controlling interest in multinational business, vast land holdings, agribusiness, media, and colleges, with assets exceeding 30 billion U.S. dollars.[3] A recent letter to LDS church leaders and congregations in the United States urged members to go after elected and appointed positions in all areas of political office,[4] thus extending church influence into every facet of government on both the local and national levels.

Mormons are no longer viewed as an isolated group of people with curious beliefs. Their temples, stakes, wards, and branches* are prominent landmarks in cities around the world.

Together this growth and influence make Mormonism a formidable challenge to Christian evangelism and ministry. This book is intended to help meet this challenge by contrasting the major beliefs and practices of the LDS branch of Mormonism with those of Christianity and showing what Christians can do evangelistically in response.

---

*See "Glossary of LDS Words," page 87.

# 1

# THE CEO OF MORMONISM

HE SAT IN MY OFFICE, HEAD BURIED BETWEEN HIS HANDS.
"I hate God! That miserable old 'Tyrant'—I hate Him!" The
words punctured my sanctified eardrums. "How dare He make
my life a miserable wreck!" Tears began to fill his eyes. "Who
is He? I . . . I just don't know who He is. What gives Him the
right?" His words trailed off.

Martin had spent 60 years of his life a devout Mormon, a
temple worker and member of the Melchizedek Priesthood.
He was steeped in a tradition that stretched over three gener-
ations of Mormon ancestors. His great-grandfather had gone
to Salt Lake Valley with the first handcart company of pio-
neers destined to establish a Mormon empire west of the
Wasatch front.

Martin didn't really hate God. He was confused and could
not force himself to focus his hurt and anger on the church or
its leadership. One of the most sacred covenants repeated
during the Mormon temple ceremony is that the covenant
participant will never speak against the leadership of the
church on pain of death.

There was more in Martin's denial. Martin's father and
grandfather had been influential leaders in the Salt Lake City
business and church communities. He respected and loved
them. To speak against them, even though they had been
stern and abusive, was a breach of his duty as a son. Martin
felt helpless. He felt robbed and deprived of his personhood.
This dissatisfaction stemmed from a love-hate relationship he
had long endured with his family and church. At all costs to
his person Martin was duty-bound to protect both the patri-

arch of his ancestry and the sacred trust of his church. In his
denial of family culpability a transfer had taken place. Rather
than admit that his parents or the LDS Church contributed
to the cause of his problems, he directed all of his anger and
frustration toward God.

What is there about the Mormon religion that encourages
their believers to equate the practices of abuse and repression
to the character of God? This could only happen when the
true nature of God is misunderstood. It is as if a faulty market-
place scale falsely labeled as God's is giving unjust, unrighteous, and impure results. Since the scale is believed by the
"customers" to be labeled correctly and to measure accurately,
the results are a false perception of truth. In this case it is a
false concept of God. Thus in the mind of the perceiver God
becomes unjust, unrighteous, and impure. It is not a true
recording; rather, it is a false discernment.

Joseph Smith, the founder and first president of the
Church of Jesus Christ of Latter-day Saints, taught, "God
himself was once as we are now, and is an exalted man, and
sits enthroned in yonder heavens!"[1] This teaching was amplified by Orson Hyde, who on October 6, 1853, instructed his
listeners to "remember that God, our Heavenly Father, was
perhaps once a child, and mortal like we ourselves, and rose
step by step in the scale of progress, in the school of advancement; has moved forward and overcome, until He has arrived
at the point where He is now."[2]

Martin's reluctance to reverence such a god* is not surprising. In this context "Heavenly Father" is not much different from us humans. The major variance is that he has been
elevated to a "corporate headquarters" where he becomes the

---

*Throughout the remainder of this book a stylistic distinction will
be made between terms referring to Mormon deities and those referring to the God of Judeo-Christianity. With some exceptions, pro-
nouns and the word "god" will not be capitalized when they refer to
the former.

"CEO" of this particular planet. Thus all of his peers, who made their way through the ranks, are today producing spiritual babies on millions of other planets scattered about the universe. If Martin were to do his best, he might someday have a shot at being in the same corporate setting as Heavenly Father. His promotion would be to some other planet, but who decides his destination is somewhat unclear. Thus in reality Martin finds himself in competition with Heavenly Father. Any feeling that this god is messing up Martin's life raises the suspicion of interference with his ambitions for potential godhood.

There isn't a court of appeals to which he can address his grievances beyond Heavenly Father. There is no structure that identifies a link with other gods in charge of planets outside our own. Nor is there a heavenly chain of command leading back to the "head" god who started it all. Brigham Young taught that this progression of gods has always been and will always continue.

It appears that when a Mormon achiever is awarded his godhood, he will become autonomous on his own planet— separate from all others. This is more clearly seen when examining the composition of the council of gods that Mormons claim gathered to decide the fate of planet Earth. This council consisted of Heavenly Father and members of his own family who had achieved a "noble and great" status in the preexistence. No identity is given of any other gods that were supposedly present. Thus with regard to Martin's potential godhood, interference in any way by Heavenly Father can be construed as unfair competition. Martin is truly alone in all his striving.

His wife cannot help him. In order to achieve Celestial glory the Mormon woman must have a Mormon man who holds the priesthood. This man must call her into his station of eternity. Her calling forth is done by using the new and secret name assigned her during the temple endowment and sealing ceremony. The purpose of the new name is so that the bride and any other wives her husband may choose[3] will be secluded onto some distant planet where he will duplicate with them Heavenly Father's services of procreating spirit babies for all eternity. Mormon teaching reveals that in the preexistence there are multiple gods, each with numerous wives. From each of the gods, there are countless sons and daughters born as spirit babies. The number of these offspring is beyond count because each parent is in a condition to produce off-spring for all eternity.

Some time ago I had lunch at the Sky Room restaurant on the campus of Brigham Young University (BYU) with a law professor of that institution named John Welch. Dr. Welch is the founder of the Foundation for Ancient Research and Mormon Studies (FARMS) as well as the editor of the BYU Studies Journal on Mormon theology. During our conversation I asked Dr. Welch, "Were all gods once humans before being elevated to godhood? If so, who was the first god?" He alluded to the book *Doctrine and Covenants*, which is the third canon of Mormon scripture, by saying, "The intelligence of man is, in some sense, coeternal with God." Thus he dismissed my question as being a "moot point."

What Dr. Welch suggested is a Mormon doctrine found at the very heart of Mormonism. Confirming that doctrine, James Talmage wrote: "We believe in a God who is himself progressive, whose majesty is intelligence; whose perfection consists in eternal advancement—a being who has attained His exalted state by a path which now His children are permitted to follow, whose glory it is their heritage to share."[4]

As this Mormon doctrine evolved, Orson Pratt built upon Smith's revelations by reasoning that "God, the Father of our spirits, became the Father of our Lord Jesus Christ according to the flesh. . . . He [God] had a lawful right to overshadow the Virgin Mary in the capacity of a husband, and beget a Son, although she was espoused to another; for the law which He gave to govern men and women was not intended to govern himself, or to prescribe rules for His own conduct."[5]

Here Pratt suggests that Heavenly Father was justified in his incestuous relationship with his spirit-born daughter whose earthly name was Mary. His teaching, however, makes this god a radical who can negate his holiness and pursue whatever lifestyle he desires for himself. This doctrine has far-reaching implications. It infers that the future estate of all who are found worthy to become gods will be free from restraint. Such gods can make whatever laws they desire, and fashion them after their own personal lusts. In this rationale such a god's majesty is reduced to knowledge. He may then adjust that knowledge to fit his own desires.

Mormon theologians are now defining the intelligence of a human as the essence of his or her being. They conclude that the soul, spirit, person, and whatever else making up the personality of a man or woman are temporary. In contrast, Mormon intelligence is linked with the eternal essence of all things. Mormon intelligence is thus distinct from character and holiness. Accordingly, lesser identities will pass away, but the intelligence will coexist with the eternal. Mormonism reduces the essential nature of humankind to knowledge. In the Garden of Eden the suggestion of Satan was that through knowledge Adam and Eve could achieve equality with God.

Knowledge is a system of works designed to achieve freedom from the constraints of mortality. In relying upon knowledge humans are thrust into competition not only with God but with each other as well. Present-day Mormon apostle M. Russell Ballard, in his book *Our Search for Happiness*, alludes to the origin of humans who populate the earth by saying it "goes back . . . to a time when we all lived as the spiritual children of our Heavenly Father. We didn't have physical bodies of flesh and bones as we now have, but the essence of our being—our spiritual selves, if you will—existed along with the rest of our Heavenly Father's spirit children."[6]

Yet for Christians God's majesty is not intelligence. He is omniscient, omnipotent, and omnipresent, but His majesty is none of these. God's majesty is holiness, purity, and perfection. The writer of Hebrews said, "Without holiness no one will see the Lord" (12:14). A few verses earlier the writer records that "God disciplines us for our good, that we may share in his holiness" (v. 10). Sharing is a condition of relationship. In Isa. 6:3 the prophet is suddenly brought to see the throne of God. His eyes were opened to the majesty of God Almighty with the words "Holy, holy, holy is the LORD Almighty." When God's holiness is undermined, then the character of God is maligned.

The Bible teaches that God is the same yesterday, today, and forever. He never changes. The holy character that He prescribes for all humankind is His very nature. The rules that He envisions for humankind are the very rules that He demands of himself. If this fails to be a consistent truth, then God cannot be trusted with human salvation.

Throughout the following chapters we will see that the Mormon misperception of God is at the heart of Mormonism's deviation from biblical Christianity. From this faulty view come distortions involving the Scriptures, revelation, ministry, and most importantly salvation. As we have seen in the case of Martin, these distortions can result in a spiritually corrosive outlook. What Martin and others like him need is someone to tell them what the true God is really like and to show them the freedom, love, purity, and holy wonder of a life lived in communion with Him. Reaching people like Martin is the goal; showing what our all-loving, all-powerful, holy God is like through our words and lives is the way.

# 2

# MARKS OF THE CULT

WE MAY RESTATE OUR TWOFOLD INQUIRY into Mormonism as follows: first, to determine if Mormonism is another form of Christianity or a cult and, second, to outline a strategy for an effective witness to those of the LDS persuasion. It seems many are attracted to the cult, the occult, and other forms of worship that are not traditional or orthodox Christianity. David Breese wrote:

> The prevailing emotion of this civilization is not love or hate or anything so activistic, it is boredom. We demand new fascinations to feed our ever-shortening spans of interest. This demand for new fascinations has led many to try to move beyond the faith once delivered to the saints to something newer (and therefore presumably truer) and more exciting.[1]

*Webster's Ninth New Collegiate Dictionary* defines a cult as "religion regarded as unorthodox or spurious." "Spurious" is defined as being "of illegitimate birth." Thus the Evangelical understanding of a cult is an unorthodox religion whose origins are derived from principles or persons that are not authentic sources to represent what that religion claims to represent.

A cult is a religious perversion (a turning from the right way). It is a belief and practice in the world of religion that calls for devotion to a religious view or leader centered in false doctrine. It is an organized heresy. A cult may take many forms, but it is basically a religious movement that distorts or warps orthodox faith to the point where truth becomes perverted into a lie. A cult is impossible to define except against the absolute standard of the teaching of Holy Scripture.

When contrasted to biblical truths, a cult is seen to have distinguishing marks by which it can be labeled as being fatally sub-Christian.

Paul wrote for our edification: "The Spirit clearly says that in later times some will abandon the faith and follow deceiving spirits and things taught by demons" (1 Tim. 4:1).

Why would an individual leave the truth and align with a false religion? Honest answers may help church leaders detect deficiencies in discipleship that leave members dissatisfied or "bored," as Breese suggests. Using the Bible as my inspiration, I have defined five areas of deviation from biblical orthodoxy that portray the marks of a cult.

1. The person and authority of God is diminished.

2. The authority and accuracy of Scripture is questioned to allow for new revelation that supplants biblical precepts.

3. The pregrace condition of humankind is not that of being hopelessly lost.

4. Jesus Christ is not the only way to God.

5. Humankind is not dependent entirely upon Christ's atonement but can achieve some form of salvation through personal merit.

Utilizing these five points, I will attempt to compare the LDS faith with biblical standards and then prescribe a remedy to bring about healing.

Before beginning we must understand the significant gulf that separates Mormonism from mainstream Christianity. In writing to the believers at Ephesus Paul offers an eye-opening glimpse into the struggle that confronts all efforts to witness for Jesus Christ: "For our struggle is not against flesh and blood, but against the rulers, against the authorities, against the powers of this dark world and against the spiritual forces of evil in the heavenly realms" (Eph. 6:12).

In 1834 Joseph Smith recalled in his journal that at the age of 14 "a thick darkness gathered around me, and it seemed to me for a time as if I were doomed to sudden destruction. . . . just at this moment of great alarm, I saw a pillar of light exactly over my head. . . . It no sooner appeared than I found myself delivered from the enemy which held me bound. . . . I saw two Personages . . . standing above me in the air. One of them spake unto me, calling me by name and said, pointing to the other—'This is My Beloved Son. Hear Him!'"[2]

On at least six separate occasions following that first encounter Joseph Smith claimed to have been visited by biblical personalities. Whether Mormonism is Christian or non-Christian hinges in part on the answer to the question, "Did Smith have physical encounters with Heavenly Father, Jesus Christ, John the Baptist, Elias, Elijah, Moses, Peter, James, John, and various angels in the vicinity of Palmyra, New York, and at Kirtland, Ohio?"

The LDS claim that Smith was empowered in his writing and preaching by heaven's authority underlies the very foundation of Smith's focus on rescuing Christianity from its supposed apostasy. Smith claimed that the true gospel was abandoned and lost following the death of the original apostles.[3] The reason the heavenly beings had singled Smith out was to restore the gospel, and the message communicated to him is the sole source from where all LDS doctrines and practices originate. The restoration thus came following the publication of the *Book of Mormon* and the reintroduction of the Aaronic and Melchizedek Priesthoods.

Smith was not alone during many of these heavenly visitations. For example, Mormon documents record that Oliver Cowdery and Joseph Smith were together when visited in 1829 by John the Baptist, who appeared to confer on them the priesthood of Aaron. Cowdery, who later turned from Smith in disillusionment, continued to confirm the authenticity of that particular visitation even after parting company from Smith.[4]

Several alternatives surface here: (1) Joseph Smith was visited and commissioned by Jesus Christ to restore the true gospel; (2) Joseph Smith and others imagined or made up everything that happened, and he built his entire life and the LDS faith upon that fabrication; or (3) Joseph Smith and others were indeed visited by beings masking their true identity. The apostle Paul warns in 2 Cor. 11:14-15 that "Satan himself masquerades as an angel of light. It is not surprising, then, if his servants masquerade as servants of righteousness."

Clearly whatever might be the source of these experiences, if the teachings derived from them are contrary to the teachings of the Bible, then we are confronted with forces or influences offering a gospel unlike that of the New Testament. Again in Gal. 1:8 Paul cautions that "even if we or an angel from heaven should preach a gospel other than the one we preached to you, let him be eternally condemned!"

We need more than mere argument to counter these influences. As Paul exhorted in Eph. 6, this is not a fight "against flesh and blood." We are not called to bash and batter Mormons. We are fighting spiritual influences that are just beyond our fingertips and just outside of our abilities to control. Our own power of reason is not enough to overpower these influences. Only in the power of the indwelling Spirit of the living Christ can our efforts prove successful.

When my wife and I first went into the Utah Valley to resurrect and pastor a church, we prayed and solicited the prayers of some 300 people across the United States. That was the first step in our strategy. We realized that the enemy was not our Mormon neighbors but a pantheon of spiritual influences that were vying for control of the minds of men and women much as was the intent of the serpent in the Garden of Eden.

We held fast to our faith in Jesus Christ, and our Lord came forth with complete victory over all the spiritual influences. We knew that the victory we experienced was not ours but the Lord's and the successes we experienced were not due to our own efforts but to those of Jesus, whose life was lived in perfect obedience to the will of the Father. We also knew that our faith was measured by our faithfulness in righteous living. Thus we sought with all our hearts to live the kind of testimony only Jesus could live through us. Mentally, morally, emotionally, and spiritually our lives were joined to Him, and in His strength we entered upon the Utah mission field victors before we even started.

Such prayer-infused preparation and obedience must comprise the first step to reaching those entangled by the influences of Mormonism. Only when we prayerfully submit our ministries and ourselves to God, can others more clearly see the God-empowered validation of the Christian gospel over any other.

# 3

# THE PLURALITY OF GODS

IF GOD IS NOT THE SOVEREIGN GOD, above all else, independent of any control or influence, then God is not the one true God at all but some lower form of being who masquerades as God. The first objective of a cult is to discredit God or diminish His authority. As for Joseph Smith, early in his career he belittled the person of God and preached the plurality of gods. On one occasion he said, "Many men say there is one God; the Father, the Son and the Holy Ghost are only one God. I say that is a strange God anyhow—three in one, and one in three! It is a curious organization."[1]

Smith confused the person of God when he declared that both the Father and the Son had bodies of bone and flesh, while the Holy Ghost alone was composed of spirit and was thus the only one to reside within a mortal human being.

Probably the most sensational statement that Joseph Smith uttered had to do with the person of God and the potential of humankind when he said, "You have got to learn how to be gods yourselves, and to be kings and priests to God, the same as all gods have done before you."[2]

To bring God down to the level of humankind and elevate humans to the level of God has only one parallel in the Christian Bible and that is in the temptation of Satan as recorded in Gen. 3. It is the eternal quest of Satan to lure the human creation into believing that God is nothing more than a hindrance to the human potential of achieving godhood.

In the past century Bruce McConkie (LDS apostle, historian, and theologian) attempted to clarify Mormon thought on this subject and wrote: "Father, Son, and Holy Ghost comprise the Godhead. As each of these persons is a God, it is evident, from this standpoint alone, that a *plurality of gods* exists."[3]

Twisting scripture is a trademark of the cult, and Joseph Smith was not beyond that kind of manipulation to force his ideas into scriptural texts. He, in reading the Book of Genesis, attempted to translate the Hebrew word *reshiyth*, which is translated "in the beginning," as "the head" and made it say, "The head of the gods called the gods together."[4]

Smith corrupted the meaning of the Hebrew word *reshiyth*, which refers to a beginning before or above any other. The word refers to the head as a part of the body, above all else in the body.[5] There is no reference here to the head god among other gods nor is there such a concept found anywhere else in the Bible. The meaning refers to the first cause, where there was nothing before. It is a starting point above all else.

As the reasoning of LDS thinkers sought to describe the conditions of God, their reasoning decided that every son has a father, and since Jesus Christ is the Son of God, it was only natural to conclude that the Father also had a father before himself and his father a father. For McConkie this boils down to the conclusion that "in this way both the Father and the Son, as also all exalted beings, are now or in due course will become gods of gods."[6]

McConkie's assumption that there are gods over gods over gods over gods contradicts the very meaning of God. A young man who had recently converted out of the LDS religion testified that the event that arrested his belief in Mormonism occurred during a high school seminary class. He said that he began to question the concept of a succession of gods. He said that he asked his teacher if God had a grandfather. "My conclusion," declared the student, "was that nothing can predate God—He is the first, last, and only God" (see Isa. 43:10-11). By His very nature God must predate everything else. There can be no person or thing coeternal with God. If there are two gods, the two will be in competition with each other. God is the uppermost or, in the former situation, the Creator, even the Head above all the body. There cannot be two heads, each over the other. Either one will rise above the other, or they will both go down struggling. If God is God, there can be no other God. Even in Greek mythology the ancients realized that there had to be a prime mover or first cause. Anything that predates or is more powerful or more knowledgeable than God would itself be God. Thus, every grandfather of God is God and the child cannot be God as long as his father exists. For the grandfather to cease to exist would render him mortal. Thus God cannot have either a father or a grandfather.

Some time ago I was escorted by Elder Preator through the Mormon visitors' center located in Independence, Missouri. Brother Preator explained all of the pictures and displays, then answered many of my probing questions with patience and reserve. When we came to a certain point in the tour, he was explaining the differences between the three degrees of glory that a Mormon can expect following the resurrection. When he had finished his presentation, I asked, "I have heard that out in Utah the LDS Church has this huge vault up in the mountains where they keep all the records of family genealogies and church membership and things like that. Why do you go to all the expense and trouble to keep these records in that remote vault in the side of the canyon?"

Brother Preator replied without any hesitation, "We cannot expect god to keep track of all the billions of people on the earth. So he has to delegate this task to the mortal priests."

Preator's response is exactly where the working out of a Mormon philosophy of deity leads. A Mormon god is a man who has human weaknesses. A Mormon god is not the first cause, but rather an engineer who fashions out of the materials available a new structure and design. To Mormon reasoning we, who are human, originated in a god who had a father and grandfather. The essence of that origin remains in us. Thus to conclude that this god needs that part of his cointelligence that we possess to keep track of things does not seem farfetched at all.

Brigham Young University (BYU) professor James E. Ford wrote in 1980 that according to Mormon doctrine "we [Mormons] are not dependent upon God for our existence."[7] Such an argument is so aligned with Satan's deception to Eve in the Genesis record that it nearly carries his signature of authenticity. The Genesis record reveals that it was the breath of God that made the human a living being, not Heavenly Father's cohabitation with some spiritual goddess (see Gen. 2:7). The apostle Paul wrote: "In him we live and move and have our being" (Acts 17:28).

The Mormon god is not the God of the Bible. This is the central truth that alienates Mormonism from mainstream Christianity. The picture of a Mormon god presents the same god-shaped lure that Satan dangled before Adam and Eve. It was the result of their succumbing to Satan's temptation that God Almighty cast them out of His presence. Humankind's own decision to rebel brought upon the human race the plight of sin. Sin is the cause of our spiritual alienation and condemnation.

Mormons commonly refer to the god of this world as "Heavenly Father" (Elohim). Mormons believe that Jesus is one of Heavenly Father's spirit sons. They call Him "The Savior." Satan was another spirit child, and for that matter, so is each man and woman born upon this earth. Thus, Heavenly Father is our spirit father, the spirit father of Jesus and also of Satan. This filial relationship makes all of these entities— human beings, Jesus, Satan, all the demons of hell, and all the angels of heaven—spirit brothers and sisters.

The writer of Isaiah records these words of Yahweh: "Before me no god was formed, nor will there be one after me. I, even I, am the Lord, and apart from me there is no savior" (43:10-11).

# 4

# UNFOLDING THE PAGES
# OF REVELATION

SATAN'S CRAFTY SUGGESTION TO EVE WAS, "Did God really say, 'You must not eat from any tree in the garden'?" (Gen. 3:1). Joseph Smith's equally crafty suggestion to this generation of Eve's children declares that the Bible has been corrupted. In the *Book of Mormon* Smith wrote that "after the book [Bible] hath gone forth through the hands of the great and abominable church, that there are many plain and precious things taken away from the book."[1]

M. Russell Ballard, a current LDS general authority,* writes that "although the early apostles worked hard to preserve the church that Jesus Christ left to their care and keeping, they knew their efforts would eventually be consumed by crisis. . . . [By A.D. 325] the Church organized by the Savior had disappeared from the earth."[2] Mormons are carefully taught that the Bible has been corrupted. They are coached that the teachings of Jesus and the original apostles were perverted to the point that everything had to be restored. Thus any teaching of the "abominable church" that contradicts LDS instruction is discounted. As a result the Bible's authority is greatly diminished in a Mormon's mind when compared to the progressive revelation given through the LDS prophets.

During the early history of Mormonism, progressive revelation accounted for the publication of *The Pearl of Great*

---

*See "Glossary of LDS Words," page 87.

Price and *The Doctrine and Covenants* as well as the *Book of Mormon*. The leaders canonized those publications, and their authority is supreme in Mormon doctrine. Subsequent to the original publication of the *Book of Mormon* many corrective revelations have changed LDS practices. The two most no-table are the rescinding of polygamy and awarding to Blacks access to the priesthood. When the books of Mormon were first canonized, these teachings were rooted in eternal prac-tices. However, the "living prophet," who is currently LDS President Gordon B. Hinckley, can reveal or rescind revela-tion as God speaks through him.

The issue of biblical credibility is crucial. Only a verifiable confidence in the Word of God can settle the question of whose authority is genuine, the Bible's or Joseph Smith's. Mormons will allege that the Bible is filled with inconsisten-cies and contradictions, while Mormon scriptures are without error. They insist that God inspires their living prophet, while Christian preachers are uninformed.

Probably the question most frequently asked by an LDS be-liever is, "How can you trust a Bible when it contains so many contradictions and obvious errors?" The basis of this question goes back to Joseph Smith's allegation that following the death of the original apostles and especially following the compro-mise of Constantine,[3] the Church diverted from its original teachings until all truth was lost. Mormons believe that the Bible itself was corrupted through faulty translation and inac-curate revision. However, the discovery of the Dead Sea Scrolls has come to our aid in responding to these assertions.

Mormon scholars place much emphasis on the Dead Sea Scrolls. They point to these manuscripts as confirming many things that are written in the *Book of Mormon*. Yet they have overlooked the most important aspect of the Scrolls. Frag-ments of every book of the Old Testament, with the excep-tion of the Book of Esther, have been recovered from the caves surrounding the Dead Sea. The most extensive of these is a complete manuscript of Isaiah. In examining these texts scholars have confirmed that the translations that occur in our modern Bibles are in essence the same as those preserved in the caves.

The impact of this intelligence is awesome. The Dead Sea Scrolls confirm the Old Testament of the Bible to be an accurate and reliable source without error in translation dating back to the first century B.C. They confirm that the very biblical texts that Jesus quoted during His lifetime are preserved for us in the exact words that He read with His eyes upon the scroll. Jesus confirmed that the Old Testament was accurate in His day. The apostles confirmed that it was the very Word of God (see 1 Tim. 3:16-17). Today, together with the New Testament, the Bible contains those same Scriptures. Thus the Bible is sufficient to examine the nature of God and determine if there is any change from what Mormons teach as it is compared with what Jesus confirmed as truth in His day.

Mormons claim the *Book of Mormon* to be translated directly from a set of golden plates unearthed by Smith from a hill near his home outside of Palmyra, New York. There has been much written about the tablets and the suspicious nature of their origin and disappearance following translation. The *Book of Mormon* has within its pages, however, many startling truths that most Mormons are unaware of. During my interview with Jack Welch on the campus of BYU I asked him about some of these discrepancies. "In the *Book of Mormon*," I said, "there are numerous references to God that describe Him as being one God in trinity." I asked, "Can you explain why this should be so when the doctrine of the LDS Church is solidly grounded in a theology of polytheism?"

This was the only question that I asked Dr. Welch for which he did not have a ready answer. After a moment of thought he said, "That's a good question. I do not believe that it has ever been researched; I may have to do that."

It is a good question. It is a question that highlights the evolution of Smith's doctrine. When he began his religion, copying much of the *Book of Mormon* directly from the King James Version of the Bible, he copied verses and principles that reflect the biblical doctrine of God as one in trinity. As

Smith's philosophy of religion progressed, he changed his concepts without blotting out previous revelations. Mormon leadership often finds embarrassment with Smith's inconsistencies and lack of writing skills. That embarrassment has caused the LDS leaders to authorize more than 4,000 changes and corrections to the *Book of Mormon* since its first publication in 1830. Smith called it the most accurate book ever written, yet its accuracy has resulted in a constant series of revisions and corrections.

In writing the eighth LDS article of faith Joseph Smith set the tone for biblical acceptance. "The Bible," he wrote, "is the Word of God as long as it is translated correctly." As a consequence Mormon interpretation of Bible passages often lead to bizarre and unrealistic conclusions. Mormon missionaries declare that the Bible has many errors, so to a person who is not familiar with the nature of the Bible's preservation a visit from those missionaries can arouse many doubts.

Mormons claim three books in addition to the Bible that comprise the complete canon of scripture. When a Mormon speaks of scripture, it is always with the understanding that the Bible is not the source of their most cherished revelation. The three books that form the heart of LDS theology and philosophy are the *Book of Mormon, The Doctrine and Covenants,* and *The Pearl of Great Price.*

Joseph Smith testified to the authority of the *Book of Mormon* in his journal on November 28, 1841, when he wrote "that the Book of Mormon was the most correct of any book on earth."[4]

Faith in Mormon teaching can be attributed to either an ignorance of the inconsistencies and contradictions that accompany LDS literature or a blinding focus upon the lie, which Satan began with Eve, that it's possible to become "like God." The biblical narrative reveals that Satan's first encounter with humans was to offer two enticements: First, Satan set out to discredit the Word of God. "'You will not surely die,' the serpent said to the woman. 'For God knows that when you eat of it [the tree of the knowledge of good and evil] your eyes will be opened'" (Gen. 3:4). Second, Satan put the carrot before the innocent couple in the garden and suggested that "you will be like God" (v. 5). These are precisely the two lures that Joseph Smith offers those who will follow him into Mormonism.

Mormon apostle Joseph B. Wirthlin, speaking before the LDS General Conference, October 6, 1996, reiterated the Mormon doctrine of an error-prone Bible that was originally voiced by Joseph Smith. Then he added that the Mormon books offer "the knowledge that Jesus Christ is the central figure of every dispensation from Adam to Joseph Smith and including President Gordon B. Hinckley."[5]

Denying the Bible's credibility opens the door for introducing new revelation designed to restore what was supposedly lost. This new revelation has the authority to supplant even the teachings of Jesus and introduce non-Christian principles into LDS theology. In scripture Jesus taught that He would send the Holy Spirit to "remind you of everything" (John 14:26). If God's Holy Spirit has the power to keep all things in remembrance and if the words spoken by Jesus that "the gates of Hades will not overcome it [the Church]" (Matt. 16:18) are true, then there was never a falling away and never a need for any restoration. Yet here the power and authority of God is in question for those who follow the Mormon belief system. For them if God was not powerful enough to protect what He had established, it would be difficult to believe any of His promises. Like the serpent in the Garden of Eden, Joseph Smith questioned the integrity of God's Word and led his followers to do likewise.

The LDS missionary climaxes his or her appeal by suggesting that the "investigator," or non-Mormon individual seeking further understanding of the LDS religion, pray for a feeling of whether the *Book of Mormon* is true. When we rely on feelings alone, our experience can be the result of desire or even a salesperson's convincing persuasion. In this sense a Mormon's faith is based upon what he or she calls a "burning in the bosom" that convinces the Mormon of the truth. That "burning" is a subjective confirmation, possibly even a self-fulfilling prophecy.

In contrast to this, the feelings that come to a person at the immediate forgiveness of all past sins and the indwelling presence of God's peace are the result of a personal relationship with God. This is a relationship confirmed by not only subjective experience but also the Church's experience down through the ages; the application of reason; and, ultimately, the authoritative definition of the Scriptures. These are the four tools used by John Wesley to clarify and confirm issues of faith and practice. In the end it is the last component, the Scriptures, that guides the other three in validating what is true.

When subjective experience alone is used to verify something, all sorts of errors can occur. The Scriptures themselves make this quite clear. Jer. 17:9 states: "The heart is deceitful above all things and beyond cure." The "heart" is a Hebrew concept encompassing, among other things, the "feelings and affections"; it is "the center of the entire man, the very hearth of life's impulse."[6] Unaided, this "center" is subject to error and corruption and is unreliable as a tool in determining truth. Feelings by themselves can seemingly confirm almost anything on the surface, but the Bible, reinforced by the Church's centuries-old witness and by reason, ascertains the truth of what lies underneath. Thus the LDS missionary is on shaky ground when he or she tries to confirm the authenticity of the *Book of Mormon* solely on the basis of an internal conviction.

The same goes when perceiving the Mormon lifestyle to be very moral and even spiritually holy. After all, Jesus instructed the Church that "each tree is recognized by its own fruit. People do not pick figs from thornbushes or grapes from briers. The good man brings good things out of the good stored up in his heart, and the evil man brings evil things out of the evil stored up in his heart" (Luke 6:44-45). As with the case of subjective experience, a look must be made at what underlies the surface, what beliefs motivate the actions. For the Christian, if these beliefs disagree with the Scriptures, then the lifestyle loses ground as evidence of Mormonism's validity.

In her book *No Regrets, How I Found My Way out of Mormonism*, Judy Robertson underscores how easy it is to be misled. When Judy was asked, "How were you lured into Mormonism? . . . Didn't you study the Bible?" she responded, "Well, no, we didn't. We were vulnerable to the beautiful package the LDS Church presents. Its members are the finest people you'll ever meet."[7] This admission of biblical ignorance seems to be quite common among many who accept Mormonism. Such people need to know they can experience a genuine, loving, and forgiving relationship with the one and only God—the God of the Bible. They must be shown that the Christian message is reliable; it has been confirmed not only by personal experience but also by the Church's age-old experience and by clear reasoning. Because of this the biblical witness authoritatively outweighs the contradictory messages found in the writings of Mormonism.

# 5

# HUMANITY'S CONDITION AFTER THE FALL

ACCORDING TO MORMON TEACHING, before each mortal human baby is conceived in the womb of an earthly mother, the spirit of that baby has been born in the preexistence. Joseph Smith, on May 6, 1833, at Kirtland, Ohio, said, "Man was also in the beginning with God. Intelligence, or the light of truth, was not created or made, neither indeed can be."[1]

McConkie amplified this to reveal that "matter or element is self-existent and eternal in nature, . . . and if there had been no self-existent spirit element, there would have been no substance from which those spirit bodies could have been organized."[2]

Here in a premortal existence God the Father (Elohim) established his home on a planet where he called his wives to perform eternal sex. From this spiritual sex were conceived (and continue to be conceived) spirit children. These spirit children were unable to advance into godhood in their preexistent condition. Thus Heavenly Father was responsible for preparing a world for them where they would be given the opportunity to advance as he and his father before him were given the opportunity in some distant and unknown world. We, who are of the human race, were conceived by Celestial sexual relations between Heavenly Father and his many Celestial wives. Heavenly Father, like all exalted Mormons, called his wives out of their graves from a former world. In this world he and many other human beings had worked out their mortal existence to become gods and goddesses and thereby continue the cycle of life that has repeated itself throughout eternity without beginning or end.

The purpose that rests behind all existing creation is a progression and testing to bring each of the preexistent off-spring into a worthiness of being accepted for noble service. In the *Pearl of Great Price*, Smith notes that many, including Abraham, were chosen to be rulers before their mortal birth.[3] Others who were so foreordained included Adam and Noah. From the *Doctrine and Covenants*, Smith related that Jesus Christ, being the firstborn, was also the mightiest of these no-ble and great children.[4] Each had a role to play in the progres-sion of God's plan for his spirit-born children.

From this preexistence Heavenly Father sent Adam to the earth. Adam was one of the "noble and great" ones of the preexistence. Adam's task on earth was to prepare the way for all of Heavenly Father's spirit children to attain mortality so that they may have the opportunity to qualify for godhood. The temptation in the Garden of Eden was to solicit from Adam's freedom the choice to accept the pain of mortality rather than remain immortal. To choose mortality was a com-passionate decision that would pave the way for all of his brothers and sisters in the preexistence to attain mortality and thus open the door to Celestial godhood. Adam was pre-ordained to make this choice, yet he had free agency and could have chosen the selfish route had he not been the "no-ble" person he was. His choice, rather than being a despicable Fall that alienated the human race from God and brought up-on the world a curse of damnation, was a choice that all of the children of the preexistence applauded as the right and proper choice.

The result of Adam's choice to eat of the forbidden fruit changed his existence from spirit (without blood in his veins) to mortal (humanity as we know it today). This change al-lowed humankind to progress in this mortal life for the pur-pose of achieving immortality. Those whose lives are proved worthy are destined to attain exaltation or salvation in the Celestial kingdom, where they, too, may achieve the status of becoming gods of their own worlds. In this Celestial world each god will call all of his wives out of their graves to a life of perpetual sex and pregnancy so that they can populate another planet somewhere in space.

For our planet Heavenly Father sent his preexistent children Adam and Eve to inhabit the bodies of flesh and bone. This body was not yet mortal. In its premortal condition there was no blood flowing; it would not grow old nor could it produce children. To make it possible for mortal childbirth (the ultimate purpose of mortality in order to provide earthly bodies for spirit sons and daughters that they may have the potential to become gods if they so perfected themselves) a change had to take place in the bodies of both Adam and Eve. That change could only be achieved if they disobeyed Heavenly Father's command not to eat of the tree of the knowledge of good and evil.

Adam has a special place in LDS teaching as the head of the human race and is also known to be the archangel Michael. He is said to hold a position of authority over the spirits of all humankind.

Mormonism links the office of Adam to that of Jesus. Submerged in this confusion is the LDS belief that Jesus came only to pay for Adam's sin. This is amazing because according to Mormon theology Adam was preinstructed to fall in the garden so that humankind could become mortal and thus prepare the preexistent spirit children of Heavenly Father for their future potential to become gods in their own right. The mechanics of this plan was designed so that the spirit babies born to Heavenly Father in the preexistence could be sent to earth and live in mortal bodies. Nelson writes that "the Fall of Adam constituted the mortal creation and brought about the required changes in their bodies, including the circulation of blood and other modifications as well. They were now able to have children."[5] According to Mormon thinking, the only purpose of humankind is to reproduce babies whether in heaven or on earth.

LDS teaching removes even the act of creation from God.

Working this reasoning out to its logical conclusion, it would seem that God is merely a "nice guy" according to Mormon belief. He did not truly create, for matter is coeternal with the intelligence of God and humans. Humans were born through spiritual sex between Elohim and his many wives, and the mortality of humankind is a result of Adam's decision to eat of the forbidden fruit in the garden. The Mormon male is in a process of working his way into godhood. The female is destined to become the spirit mother of unnumbered children conceived through spiritual sex and painful birth throughout the endless ages of eternity.

According to this belief, the human race is not lost as a result of sin. The deeds men and women do are not condemning but stratifying. There is no condemnation or hell. With the exception of the sons of perdition and the angels who followed Lucifer into rebellion, everyone will fit snugly into one of Smith's three heavens where he or she will live happily ever after. Status in these heavens is dependent not upon the grace of God but upon the works of a person's own hands. Brigham Young wrote and taught that "there is not a man or woman who violates covenants made with their God that will not be required to pay the debt. The blood of Christ will never wipe that out. Your own blood must atone for it."[6]

In contrast to Mormon teaching the apostle Paul wrote that there is none who are righteous; all people are sinners in need of reconciliation with God (see Rom. 3:9-18, 23; 6:23). The result of human rebellion is human depravity. In their desire to avoid God, people have tried to establish their own righteousness. Isaiah calls our righteous acts nothing more than "filthy rags" (see Isa. 64:6). The provision of Jesus' death and resurrection is to open the door for all men and women who repent of their sins and trust in Christ to receive eternal life. This salvation is without cost, without personal atonement, and without works. To Martha, the sister of Lazarus, Jesus said, "I am the resurrection and the life. He who believes in me will live, even though he dies; and whoever lives and believes in me will never die" (John 11:25-26). Paul writes that "we also rejoice in

God through our Lord Jesus Christ, through whom we have now received reconciliation" (Rom. 5:11).

To reconcile something is to bring it back to its original condition. Reconciliation is in the present tense. Christians are now reconciled to God through Jesus Christ. Reconciliation is in this life and becomes effective upon receiving Jesus through faith. It is not in some hoped-for eternity when our good deeds will be measured against our bad deeds as we stand before Joseph Smith, who screens us before being judged by Jesus Christ and Heavenly Father. In truth God has already justified those who are born of the Spirit through faith, and we are sealed by the Holy Spirit of God who comes to dwell within us (see Eph. 3:17; 4:30).

# 6

# IMMORTALITY AND EXALTATION

MORMONISM AND BIBLICAL ORTHODOXY PART COMPANY in two final areas. First, for Mormons salvation consists of several forms that are not limited to the work of Jesus Christ. Second, one such form requires personal merit.

Unlike Christians, Mormons consider Jesus' atonement on the Cross to be inadequate because they believe He was taken there against His will. They believe the voluntary atonement was the incident in the Garden of Gethsemane where sweat drops of blood were shed for Adam's race. To them the atonement on the Cross is limited solely to resurrecting all humans from the dead. This resurrection is to immortality but not to salvation. Through immortality all are guaranteed eternal life in a place that is better than the earth we live in today. Salvation or exaltation is reserved for those people whose life here on earth is deemed worthy. For everyone else, immortality moves them into either the Terrestrial or Telestial heaven— the two lower levels in a three-tiered system; to get into the highest heaven, the Celestial, you must be a temple-worthy Mormon.* Those who work their way into the Celestial kingdom will be with Heavenly Father and "The Savior," who is their Jesus Christ. Those in the lower heavens will be cut off from this Celestial relationship. In this way Joseph Smith designed a heaven all his own.

---

*For a detailed description of this heavenly system see chapter 8, pages 53-57.

Mormons teach that salvation is by grace after the seeker of salvation has done everything he or she can do on his or her own. There is a serious difference in the teaching of the Bible and the teaching of the LDS community. McConkie relates that "under certain circumstances there are some serious sins for which the cleansing of Christ does not operate, and the law of God is that men must then have their own blood shed to atone for their sins."[1]

Satan told Eve that she would not die if she ate of the forbidden fruit—but then Satan is a liar. As a result of believing Satan's lie, Mormons think the entire human race is on the quest to attain equality with God (which is self-sufficiency and independence from the demands of God on one's life). This quest places each man in competition with God. The pressure to achieve becomes so intense that many individuals end up living a lie. They have found in their own strength that they are unable to meet Heavenly Father's requirements of obedience. They realize that they cannot keep all the rules. They cannot imagine why their weaknesses are so persistent. That brings on tremendous feelings of guilt.

The level of immortal attainment depends on a person's works here in this life. Jesus' atonement was to bring finality to Adam's decision in the Garden of Eden. As described earlier, that decision made all humans mortal and able to bear children. They further believe that Christ's atonement in the Garden of Gethsemane freed Adam's entire race to gain immortality. Yet it did not provide a means of forgiveness for our individual sins. For that we must each work out our own salvation by either our works or the shedding of our own blood. Then, after death, those who have not had opportunity to respond to the Mormon gospel will be sorted into what is called Spirit Prison. Here "good" Mormons from paradise will come to present the gospel. These departed saints in paradise receive their invitation to witness as a result of the prayers and baptisms for the dead performed in present-day Mormon temples.

Somehow paradise seems like an extended mission where Mormons will go out two by two into the Spirit Prison and present the gospel that they have learned at the Missionary Training Center here on earth. Those in prison may respond favorably and at that time be elevated in their eternal rank. Others will await the resurrection to the Telestial kingdom that is reserved for the lowest level of achievers.

To a Mormon, salvation has two distinct elements. First there is the doctrine of salvation by grace alone. This applies to everyone in the mere act of being resurrected after death. It is a universal resurrection into a condition of immortality.

Second is a conditional salvation that is limited to an individual's obedience to the gospel. It is here that an inheritance in the Celestial kingdom is in view. McConkie relates that "this kind of salvation follows faith, repentance, baptism, receipt of the Holy Ghost, and continued righteousness to the end of one's mortal probation."[2]

A lingering conclusion of the Mormon doctrine of salvation is that to preach a salvation by grace alone without obedience as a prerequisite to salvation, such a doctrine would tend to make the adherent lazy and apathetic to any determination of obedience to the laws of God. A works-oriented salvation places a burden of proof upon the member, while grace alone leaves one free to do much as he or she pleases. In this concept the Mormon thinking has not seriously considered the implications of love and thanksgiving for the tremendous sacrifice that God has wrought in His act of redemption. Of course, a theology that denies the effects of the Fall has no need for a full understanding of humankind's dilemma of being eternally lost and unable to bridge the gap without the shedding of innocent blood.

A works-oriented salvation leaves most people wanting. In an attempt to resolve this problem a philosophy of prayer and baptism for the dead developed. This practice is based upon the Bible teaching to the church at Corinth where Paul writes that "if there is no resurrection, what will those do who are baptized for the dead?" (1 Cor. 15:29). The LDS Church practices a baptism by vicarious-proxy labor where worthy individuals can be baptized for those who have died in times

past without ever having been evangelized by an LDS repre-
sentative. This practice is considered to be the act of a just
God who would not pass judgment on anyone who had not
been offered an opportunity to accept the gospel.

Salvation in Mormonism is also distinctive in its application to women. Most of what Smith and his followers have
written is predicated upon the male dominance that he
preached and practiced. The obsession that Mormonism
holds with eternal sex, polygamy here on earth, and racial
domination all stem from 19th-century male chauvinism.
Smith's relegating of women to being dependent upon and
under the full control of men is a mark of this prejudice.

Because of this, the Mormon woman must have a Mormon man holding the priesthood to call her into his station
of eternity (as has been described on pp. 9-10). This is the
only way she can expect anything more in the next life than
a routine of servanthood.

In contrast to all of this carefully constructed LDS salvation theology is the simple message of Scripture that says one
must be born again (see John 3). Being born again is a concept that caused Nicodemus to shudder at the thought of being stuffed back into his mother's womb. Jesus responded by
saying, "Flesh gives birth to flesh, but the Spirit gives birth to
spirit" (John 3:6). From the Greek text, *anōthen* (born again)
literally means to be born from above or anew. It is being
born of God through the joining of His Spirit with the spirit
of the believer. Unlike the Mormon teaching that our connection with God began with a spiritual birth in the preexistence, Paul confirms what Jesus declared to Nicodemus, that
our spiritual birth is a new condition that comes here in this
life following repentance and is evidenced by the intimate
and personal relationship believers have with the Father:

And if the Spirit of him who raised Jesus from the dead
is living in you, he who raised Christ from the dead will
also give life to your mortal bodies through his Spirit, who
lives in you. Therefore, brothers, we have an obligation—
but it is not to the sinful nature, to live according to it.

For if you live according to the sinful nature, you will die; but if by the Spirit you put to death the misdeeds of the body, you will live, because those who are led by the Spirit of God are sons of God. For you did not receive a spirit that makes you a slave again to fear but you received the Spirit of sonship. And by him we cry, "Abba, Father." The Spirit himself testifies with our spirit that we are God's children *(Rom. 8:11-16)*.

Being born anew of the Spirit of God brings us into immediate relationship with the Father as children who are redeemed from the condemnation of rebellion and sin. The gospel message teaches that "all have sinned and fall short of the glory of God" (Rom. 3:23). According to the apostle John, those outside of God's grace are lost. Those who have received the gift of God's grace are born anew and may be called Christian. There is no in-between or middle ground (see John 3:16-18).

# 7

# A STRATEGY FOR WITNESSING TO MORMONS

THE CHALLENGE FOR BELIEVERS is to understand that witnessing to Mormons is a cross-cultural experience. This means learning a new language as well as new concepts of reasoning. There are some basic rules of thumb to remember when making a cross-cultural witness. We can view these as steps that unfold one at a time. Quick "blitz" evangelism, witnessing to a person and then moving quickly on to someone or something else, will have little effect on Mormons. Leading folks out of the cultural web of cult religion takes both time and a personal long-term commitment on the part of witnessing believers.

## What Mormons Believe

Before examining the steps for Mormon evangelism, let me generalize what it is that Mormon's actually believe.

1. Mormons believe they are already Christians.

2. Mormons believe their religion is superior to all others because theirs is a restoration of the true faith lost through the apostasy that followed the death of the last original apostle. That means that they believe all church confessions other than their own are corrupted beyond help.

3. Mormons believe that their scriptures are superior to the Bible because they have a later revelation that restores those parts of the Bible lost and corrupted by the falling away of the Church.

4. Mormons believe that the living prophet (presently Gordon Hinckley) is in direct succession to the apostles ap-

pointed by Jesus and holds the key to revelation that is not present in any other church. Their prophet, through progressive revelation, can receive new inspiration from God that will supersede the revelation of the Bible and even supplant the teachings of Jesus himself.

Christianity has often sought to center its preaching and teaching on the felt needs of individuals striving to cope in this stressful world. As a result, churchgoers and readers of Christian literature are brought to an understanding of scripture that teaches how to live with one another. Professing Christians are taught love, mercy, goodness, forgiveness, tolerance, and the beatitudes of meekness and peace. All of these are essential to Christian living in our complex world. These are the very instructions that Jesus gave to the disciples. These attitudes characterize the true Church. However, the thing that many Christians do not realize is that the cults teach these very same principles and teach them very well. In fact, if one is to watch and listen closely, the moral teachings of the Mormon community often sound more Christian than what is taught by many Christian churches. Even more convincing is the outward show of good works.

To counter the threat of a Mormon flood sweeping over the heart of professing Christendom, a random study of the Bible based on contemporary or popular themes is not sufficient. There is a specific kind of biblical knowledge that is essential for preparing against the onslaught of Mormon proselytizing. The real issues that mark the difference between Mormon teachings and Christianity are found in the answers to such questions as these: Who is God? What is the condition of humankind? How is one saved? What is God's true method of revelation? Who is Jesus Christ? Can a Christian have a personal "friendship" relationship with God? When and how does one receive forgiveness? What is eternity? What does the fall of humanity signify? How does one measure sin? What is meant by heaven? What is hell? If believers are inadequately prepared to defend their beliefs in these areas, they become prime targets for Mormon evangelism.

# How to Witness to Persons of the LDS Faith

*Step One*

As we observed in chapter 2, the first step in a strategy for reaching Mormons (or any other cult members) is prayer—but not just any kind of prayer. In much of our 21st-century interpretation of spiritual warfare we have come to the place where we de-emphasize or reinterpret passages of Scripture that speak of demons. For instance, when Jesus healed the demon-possessed man who had seizures (Matt. 17:15-18), we might categorize this to be a case of a man with epilepsy. On the other hand, some people find demons in everything. They exorcize the demons of tobacco, chocolate, and whatever else appears to be addictive or dysfunctional in their lives.

While neither of these extremes seem correctly to define the spiritual condition of the demonic as described in the Bible, clearly deceptive forces exist that have an appealing influence over the affairs of men and women in this world. Whether or not we see Satan and his angels in these forces, the spiritual blindness they inflict on others by masking the gospel is quite real. We are indeed engaged in spiritual warfare. As Paul noted in Eph. 6:12, our warfare "is not against flesh and blood, but against . . . the spiritual forces of evil in the heavenly realms."

We are not saying that individual Mormons are demon possessed any more than we may say that of any other group of people. These spiritual forces have no power over an individual unless that person grants them power. Our prayer in reaching out to Mormons is to enlist the spiritual forces of God to cleanse our path that we may be fully prepared for the conflict. When the man with the seizure-afflicted son confronted Jesus, he said the disciples were unable to cast out the demon that had been tormenting his son. Jesus taught that such can only come out with "prayer and fasting" (Matt. 17:21, n.).

When the Spirit led Jesus into the wilderness to be tested, Matt. 4:2 says, "After fasting forty days and forty nights, he was hungry." The significance of Jesus' preparation for meeting temptation is an example for us all, and our preparation for spiritual warfare must not be any less. The lure that draws individuals into the cults is a subtle temptation to achieve a higher level of spiritual awareness. In the Mormon appeal for accepting their teachings we find the same ruse Satan used to bring chaos into the Garden of Eden: "For God knows that when you eat of it your eyes will be opened, and you will be like God, knowing good and evil" (Gen. 3:5). Likewise, the temptation thrown out before the prospective Mormon male is, "You can become a god if you come and follow me." Confronting such a temptation requires us to be ready.

Step one is a how-to step—how to prepare for witnessing when opposed by a spiritual blindness that hides "the light of the gospel of the glory of Christ" from those who are being deceived (see 2 Cor. 4:4). To do this we must allow the Holy Spirit full control over all of our faculties. That can only come from praying in the Spirit and fasting as modeled by Jesus during His life here on earth. When I first went to Provo to replant a church, I spent days traveling about the streets around our church building and around the grounds of the Mormon temple praying that God would unshackle the hearts of those held captive so that God's Word might penetrate into them. I prayed for the Mormon people, for those who would come to our new church, for wisdom, and for the cleansing of my motives and desires so I would wholly rely upon God's will and leadership.

Fasting and prayer put our minds and hearts in God's care. When we do this, we join with the mind of God, who leads us, not to our own inadequate human solutions, but to His solutions. Having the mind of Christ is scriptural (1 Cor. 2:16), but we must know it to have it. We can only know the mind of Christ through an unconditional surrender to His Will. Praying, fasting, and prayerfully meditating upon the Scriptures foster the self-denial and Scriptural obedience needed for such a complete surrender.

By prayer and fasting I do not necessarily mean starving

myself and cloistering my body in a closet. The spiritual significance of fasting is to consecrate my being to a cleansing process. This is where the Holy Spirit ferrets out and becomes the
replacement for all wrong thoughts and motives. It is then
God's Spirit who will direct my mind in the will of God. When
I am cleansed and purged of selfish desire, I am ready to meet
those whom God has called me to minister to. I come, not in
my own strength, but in the power of God's Holy Spirit.

In doing this I also pray using the Scriptures. It is a prayer
of meditation. It is a prayer that allows God's Word to penetrate my conscious thinking. I am now concentrating upon
the passages of Scripture where God reveals His will and
method for confronting spiritual forces. These passages become my purpose and desire. By praying the Scriptures I am
seeking both the will of God and holiness in my life. Through
prayer and fasting I am focusing upon the Source of all godly
spiritual power and opening up my life to the infilling of
God's energy and vitality.

## Step Two

Love the Mormon person, and respect his or her intelligence. Learn to separate and distinguish Mormons as individuals from Mormonism as an institution.

Contemporary Western culture has adopted a philosophy
of tolerance for all beliefs. For one to criticize another's religion is tantamount to partnership with anti-Semitism and
neo-Nazi bigotry. To cut a path through the confusion that
this pluralistic philosophy creates, a Christian must rely upon
the biblical example. Scripture reads "God so loved the world
that he gave his one and only Son" (John 3:16), yet it also
notes that the world is in opposition to God. On the one
hand, Christians are taught to love not "the world or anything in the world" (1 John 2:15), and on the other hand,
God loved the world.

It seems to be a semantical oxymoron if we assume that
God could love and not love in the same breath. Nevertheless, the answer is very simple: God loves the sinner, and Jesus

died for the sinner so that he or she may be reconciled to
God. God did not love the system or the institution. His
Word shows that in the end He will judge the world. The
world system is prophesied to end in great tribulation, and its
evil will be purged and overthrown.

By Christ's example Christians are to love cultists but acknowledge the institution for its deceit and failure. The Great
Commission asks Christians to seek the salvation of the lost
from the consequences of sin but to hate the evil that drags
men and women into the pit. Paul's example is that "I have
become all things to all men so that by all possible means I
might save some" (1 Cor. 9:22). Francis of Assisi asserted that
Christians should preach the gospel every day, in every way
that he or she can, and sometimes do it with words.

Before any witness can be effective it must carry with it a
credibility that exhibits a pattern of righteous living where
the person being witnessed to can see evidence of the power
of God. The LDS believer is generally impressed with someone whose lifestyle reflects a wholesome and godly character.
Love is evidenced in sanctified living. Love is a giving servanthood that patterns the example of Christ Jesus in a person's daily relationships with others. Love is not just a profes-
sion of the tongue. Rather it is a commitment of the heart.
Love spends time with the object of that love. Love shares af-
fection and concern. Love offers examples of service. Love is
a giving of the self without requiring anything in return.

Native American GaWaNi Pony Boy, in a book on horse
training, provides some insight into developing trust in a relationship: "Your time together is not just time when you happen to be in the same space. Hand grazing, taking a walk,
grooming (for no purpose other than to connect with your
horse), and hanging out in the pasture are all opportunities to
deepen the relationship with your horse. Barn chores, feed-
ing, and mindless longing are not."[1]

GaWaNi Pony Boy describes this "hanging out in the pasture" as being "at one" with the horse through the illustration
of an eagle soaring with the wind currents:

To understand what it means to be "one with" reflect for a moment on an eagle soaring with the currents. The eagle does not glide on top of or below or alongside those currents, but is actually enveloped within them. . . . His movements reflect the movements of the ever-shifting winds of which he has become a part. The soaring eagle knows what it means to be one with the wind.[2]

It is with this aura of "hanging out" with the other person that a trusting relationship can develop where the Mormon brother or sister can begin to feel the sincerity of a Christian witness. If the witness has not found his or her relationship with our Lord—"one with" as the soaring eagle is one with the wind—then the integrity of his or her witness may be difficult to confirm.

## Step Three

The Bible is the Christian's anchor of authority. The Bible is the Word of God. Undermining the Word of God was the serpent's tactic in the garden. It was Satan's front line of temptation against Jesus in the wilderness. It is the avenue of bringing souls into the false teachings of Mormonism. When the Bible's credibility is questioned, something else can freely replace it. A return to the Bible as the authority for all that is required for salvation is essential in combating the cultist's errors. "All Scripture is God-breathed and is useful for teaching, rebuking, correcting and training in righteousness, so that the man of God may be thoroughly equipped for every good work" (2 Tim. 3:16-17).

Mormons are carefully taught that the Bible is corrupted and that the teachings of Jesus and the original apostles were perverted to the point where everything had to be restored. Thus any teaching of the "abominable church" that is contrary to what the LDS Church supports is in error. As a result, the Bible has little jurisdiction over the progressive revelations of LDS prophets whose oracles are recorded in the *Book of Mormon, The Pearl of Great Price,* and *The Doctrine and Covenants.*

As long as a Mormon retains faith in the living prophet, there will be little movement to connect rational arguments with spiritual revelation. To them the prophet's directives as administered through the priesthood and as defined by Joseph Smith are infallible. They think the prophet speaks with the mouth of God. Thus any argument of a non-Mormon is unenlightened and unworthy of consideration. The only way to bridge this cultural gulf is to plant seeds of questioning regarding the meanings behind the words and forms of Mormon theology. The LDS prophet is the one who established the meanings. Thus until that authority is suspect, the meanings will remain unchanged.

The Mormon's armor is a conviction that the prophet speaks the words of God and that the books of Mormonism are the restored truth of God. Until a chink is wedged into this faith, until some doubt is registered in the Mormon's attitude toward these two witnesses, a believer's plea will go unheeded.

A witness before a Mormon believer must paint a clear picture of Christ's person and of the personal, intimate relationship He offers to all who come to Him believing. This is the message that transcends all the arguments of Bible proof texts. A Mormon's faith is based upon a "burning in the bosom" that convinces him or her of the truth. That "burning" is a subjective confirmation, possibly even a self-fulfilling prophecy. The language used by a Mormon to communicate his or her faith depends on the same words as that of a Christian; however, the meanings are entirely different. For the Christian such meanings spring from a personal relationship with God bringing forgiveness and the indwelling presence of God's peace. Introducing a person to this experience is the most convincing argument any witness to Mormonism can offer.

### Step Four

The fourth step in reaching Mormons is to provide a discipling network that fills the relational gap many experience in the busy church world. To do this it may be necessary to ask,

"Why do people turn to the cult?" There are those whose behavior may be labeled "cultaholic." Some require recovery groups and spiritual therapy to arrest their addiction. Others simply need a network of nurture and discipleship to give them relational security.

Mary Pipher in her book *Reviving Ophelia* writes, "Research on adolescents shows three basic motives for chemical use. The first is for expanded awareness, or the desire to increase sensitivity and insight. The second is for thrill seeking and new experiences with peers; and the third is for the drug effect—that is, to get high. All of these reasons have in common the desire to achieve an altered state of consciousness."[3] Her analysis of adolescents can be brought into religion. People seeking an altered state of consciousness leap at the tree of the knowledge of good and evil. Mormonism promises men that if they achieve a worthy character they will become gods in the next world.

Clinical research seems to confirm that once persons are caught up into addictive behaviors, the most effective way to recovery is through support groups. It is this philosophy that undergirds AA and other recovery programs. This fourth step in leading persons away from the cult includes developing the framework of recovery support where isolated and desperate individuals can come together, share common experiences, and learn how to cope with the issues that are confronting their lives. Through such recovery groups new converts also learn how to fill the vacuum in their spiritual lives through a vital relationship with God and in community with other believers.

Most important in such support groups is discipleship and nurture in biblical application and relationship, first with God and second with fellow Christians. The most flagrant failure in the church today is a dereliction in following Christ's admonition to love and support one another. A new birth requires nurture and care, and becoming part of the lives of new disciples is essential in the practice of Christianity. Many depart through the church's back door primarily because they did not experience the fullness of fellowship that Christianity promises. When church people are too busy to care, new converts lose interest quickly when left to find the way on their own.

The goal of any support group should lead those who are recovering from Mormonism to freely confess that

1. Joseph Smith and the current LDS prophet are false prophets;
2. the *Book of Mormon* contradicts the Bible and is false;
3. the LDS Church is a false religion.

# 8

# WITNESSING TO THOSE DESTINED FOR A THREE-TIERED HEAVEN

JOSEPH SMITH IDENTIFIED THREE CATEGORIES OF ETERNITY into which resurrected immortal humans would be assigned according to their worthiness following the resurrection. To some degree these three categories align with the three types of Mormons with whom a Christian will come in contact. Smith labeled the three divisions of a Mormon heaven as Celestial, Terrestrial, and Telestial. He taught that people will be sorted into these levels of heaven as a result of their conduct here in this life. Smith's labeling becomes useful in identifying the different kinds of resistance that may be expected from Mormons when confronted with the gospel.

## 1. The Celestial Believers

Celestial believers are aloof, confident, and secure in their beliefs. They are intolerant of all contrary opinion. They are the purists who see no evil, hear no evil, and speak no evil of the LDS religion. Archaeological evidence and other sources that refute Mormon claims of pre-Columbian civilizations on the American continent[1] are ignored. Evidence that confirms fraud or abuse in the character of Joseph Smith is denied. Evidence that points to misconduct by LDS leaders is pushed under the rug. When responding to accusations that there is error in LDS teachings, Celestial believers concoct some of the most farfetched stories to account for things rather than con-

sider that there could be something in their doctrine that
merits investigation

For instance, when I confronted a BYU professor about
the absence of any evidence of steel production in America
prior to the arrival of the Spanish, his response was ingenious.
He suggested that meteorites falling to the surface of the
earth undergo a process similar to steel production. "It is
probable," he said, "that the Nephites found these and fash-
ioned them into swords and shields and other items mentioned in the *Book of Mormon*." Another man was confronted
about the absence of any evidence supporting pre-Columbian
cities that are mentioned in the Book of Mormon. He responded that he had a vision revealing that these cities were
all submerged below the surface of the ocean when the land-
mass on which they were built sunk below the waters.

These are the institutional pharisees of the LDS religion.
Like their counterparts who confronted Jesus, rather than acknowledge the miracles of our Lord as being performed by
God, they are more concerned about preserving the institution and their own position within it. Celestial believers have
made up their minds. All differing opinions are moot to them.

Celestial believers may be compared with the description
Jesus offered of the Pharisees, whom He portrayed as the
blind leading the blind (see Matt. 15:12-13). Witnessing
among Celestial believers is not witnessing on receptive soil.
They, like all other people, need to hear the gospel. The example that Jesus taught the disciples in Matt. 10:14 should
apply here. When they reject the message, a Christian's response should be to move on to more receptive soil.

## 2. The Terrestrial Believers

Terrestrial believers are willing to talk. These persons
want to be accepted as Christians. They are willing to acknowledge many points of view but consider their own religion sufficient for their needs. Terrestrial believers may not be
well versed in the doctrines of their faith, but they will defend it because they trust the LDS leaders without question.
They are caught up in "doing"—committees, scouting, crafts,

office holding, and the like. Rather than discuss their faith, they feel more comfortable keeping the subject of conversation on the things they are doing. In truth the activities they do are their faith. They sincerely believe that doing will earn them merit with God.

On the whole, Terrestrial believers are not hostile to the gospel; they just don't see its importance in the overall scheme of things. They're too busy to study the Bible or other LDS literature with any degree of regularity. They don't go to church to learn about God; they go because it is a society where they can feel accepted and useful. They are obedient to the leaders and believe that their bishops and the men holding priesthood authority will guide the church into all truth. There is more receptivity among Terrestrial believers than among Celestial believers. However, strong resistance will result if the proper groundwork has not been laid with care.

### 3. The Telestial Believers

Telestial believers are more objective. They know there are serious flaws in the Mormon structure, and they are not sure what to do about it. To just up and leave the culture is frightening. The web of Mormon society ties its controlling tentacles about everything that is important in the Mormon's life—family, career, social life. Harmony in all of these areas depends on a Mormon's loyalty to the culture. Telestial believers know that things are wrong. They know that sin encroaches upon their lives. They know there has to be something better, but fear is their most powerful enemy. When confronted with a choice to receive the gospel, the fear of losing so much seems insurmountable.

The most receptive soil exists here, but to cultivate the harvest a witness must let a Mormon know what it is that will compensate for all he or she stands to lose. Jesus is the compensation, but the Jesus that Mormons have known is not sufficient. A Christian must communicate the real Jesus, and He must be communicated in a way that the Mormon can first feel and then come to believe.

## 4. The Perdition Believers—A Possible Further Category

The Perdition believers are those who are simply outcasts from all three heavenly categories. To a devout Mormon these persons are doomed. Perdition believers have a Mormon experience, but they don't believe. Yet they will defend the Mormon culture simply because there is nothing else that they know of that is worth holding on to.

When Jesus was on the earth, He identified those who were receptive, and spent much time nurturing them. He had patience and overlooked many of their failures while He taught them His way. Jesus reacted differently toward others who were hostile, rebuking the Pharisees and overturning the tables of the money changers. When a rich young ruler came to Jesus (see Matt. 19:16-22), he asked, "What must I do to gain eternal life?" Jesus said, "Keep the commandments." The young ruler said, "This I have done since my youth." Then, when Jesus told him to go and sell all he owned and follow Him, Matt. 19:22 tells us that "the young man . . . went away sad." This is a typical Mormon story. Whether it is family, business, or society, the Mormon will most often cling to the culture rather than give away all that holds him or her and follow Jesus.

In the case of the rich young ruler, our Lord did not chase after him. Instead, He let the man go. Pleadings and offering incentives would do nothing to change his mind. Conversion is a transformation of the mind that is followed by a new direction in life. The witness cannot make that kind of a change happen. Such change is only possible with the intervention of the Holy Spirit and the free will of the person who Jesus is seeking.

Few Mormons will be won over by bashing their beliefs, picketing their temples, or trashing their neighborhoods with tracts. Mormons will be won in exactly the same way all men and women are won to Christ. When they feel a need for God's presence in their lives, when they suffer a hunger for

His loving arms to enfold them, they will seek Him and they will find Him (see Jer. 29:13-14). Relationships are not built upon fear or threat, but they come out of a deep concern, out of love, and out of mutual respect.

The shield of faith absorbs the blows aimed against God's witnesses. With God's help Christians can turn the other cheek, walk the extra mile, and give from the heart with no demand for anything in return. Faith believes, offers hope, accepts the Mormon as a friend, and seeks to model the life of Christ. The Mormon will be more impressed by how Christians live their lives than by anything they say. He or she will watch and judge their Jesus by how they represent Him. Christians have the responsibility of representing the Lord in holiness, kindness, love, compassion, and faithfulness. Even the Celestial believer will be impressed by Christians whose lives are lived in holiness.

# 9

# THE MISSING LINK

Mormons are taught that they have known Heavenly Father in the preexistence but that that memory has been wiped away. The bad news is that they may never see him again. Unless Mormons are found worthy of exaltation, Heavenly Father will not be in their future. The good news is that everyone is assured immortality in some state of resurrection life. But only faithful Mormons will return to live with Heavenly Father. This hope is one prejudiced by works and not by grace. A personal relationship here in this life is impossible. A personal relationship in the life to come is problematic at best.

The central theme of witnessing to Mormons is one of bringing them to a personal relationship with the true Jesus Christ. The most enduring mark of a Christian is the indwelling presence of God in this life here and now. The relationship of Friend, Counselor, Comforter, Guide is assured to those who accept Jesus Christ as their personal Savior in this life.

In today's religious community Mormons are clamoring to be recognized as true Christians. They point to the name of Jesus in their title, the Church of Jesus Christ of Latter-day Saints, testifying that "we have a very strong belief in our Savior, Jesus Christ, who is the Head of our church." In a recent letter U.S. Senator Orrin Hatch, from the state of Utah and an LDS member, assured me that he believed "that Jesus Christ is the literal Son of God in the flesh, that He lived a perfect mortal existence, that He Atoned for the sins of all those who would repent and come unto Him. [He also assured me that he believed] that Jesus Christ was resurrected with a perfect immortal body."[1]

I do not doubt the sincerity of the senator's testimony. Only I am reminded of what the apostle Paul wrote to the believers at Corinth when he cautioned, "By this gospel you are saved, if you hold firmly to the word I preached to you. Otherwise, you have believed in vain" (1 Cor. 15:2). My prayer for all who name the name of Jesus is that in eternity they may not find they have believed in vain.

Following the election of Gordon B. Hinckley to the office of LDS president on March 12, 1995, a media blitz has been pursued to convince the world that Mormonism is just another sect of mainstream Christianity. Mormons strongly deny that they are a cult, and emphasize that the name of Jesus Christ in their title proves they are Christian. They claim that through revelation they are the restored church bringing back to the world a gospel that was lost and hidden from the historic church following the death of the original 12 apostles. Mormons teach that until that truth was revealed to Joseph Smith, there remained no authentic church in the world.

A little booklet titled *The Search for Jesus,* published by Mormon apostle Thomas Monson in 1990, presents the Mormon gospel thus:

> The shepherds of old sought Jesus the child. But we seek Jesus the Christ, our Older Brother, our Mediator with the Father, our Redeemer, the Author of our salvation; he who was in the beginning with the Father; he who took upon himself the sins of the world and so willingly died that we might forever live. This is the Jesus whom we seek.[2]

The words of this booklet sound orthodox and would appear to ably support the LDS claim to a Christian identity.

In his review of Stephen Robinson's book *Are Mormons Christians?* Brigham Young University professor of philosophy Paul Hedengren relates how Robinson approached the issue. In defense of the Mormon claim of being a Christian community Robinson enlists *Webster's Third New International Dictionary* to settle the argument. He notes that *Webster's* defines a

Christian as "one who believes or professes or is assumed to believe in Jesus Christ and the truth as taught by him." Robinson then argues that Mormons who meet this test are Christian. Commenting on Robinson's book, Hedengren observes that based on *Webster's* definition, "to deny that Latter-day Saints are Christian, one must either show that they do not believe in Jesus Christ or that they reject some truth taught by him."[3]

Clouding the issue are the words of President Gordon Hinckley, in a speech delivered at a member meeting in Paris on June 4, 1998. In his article "Thank You, Mr. President," R. Philip Roberts observes that "Hinckley stated that those outside the Church who say Latter-day Saints 'do not believe in the traditional Christ' were correct." Roberts quotes Hinckley further:

> The traditional Christ of whom they speak is not the Christ of whom I speak. For the Christ of whom I speak has been revealed in this the Dispensation of the Fullness of Times. He together with His Father, appeared to the boy Joseph Smith in the year 1820, and when Joseph left the grove that day, he knew more of the nature of God than all the learned ministers of the gospel of the ages.[4]

If then the Christ of Mormonism is not the same Christ as that of traditional Christianity, belief in the Mormon Christ has no eternal significance, since "there is no other name under heaven given to men by which we must be saved" (Acts 4:12). There is only one true Christ, and only one Christ who can save. The question is now, "How do you identify the true Christ?" The real issue here is not the definition of a Christian according to *Webster's*. The definition in *Webster's* is language centered. The meaning of any given word is relative to culture and time. Language changes, and word meanings change over time. In order to define an institution that transcends cultural boundaries, a changeless model is needed. Language does not suffice. The standard of measurement must satisfy a biblical definition that is not influenced by fluctuations in language.

Much of this reverts back to what is known as the Arian

controversy. In May of A.D. 325, the Roman emperor Constantine summoned all the bishops of the empire to the city of Nicaea in Asia Minor for what was to be the first universal council of the Church. The topic of focus was the Trinity.

Over a century earlier Tertullian of North Africa had set forth one of the first definitions of the Trinity in his debate against the Gnosticism of the second century. He held that "there is one divine 'substance' which is articulated or 'administered' into three distinct but continuous 'persons': Father, Logos/Son, and Spirit. At the same time, he offered a reflective account of the Incarnation, explaining that the person of Christ is a union of two distinct, unconfused 'substances,' divine and human, in a single 'person.'"[5]

In contrast, in the time of the Nicaean Council, Arius, a presbyter from the parish of Baucalis near Alexandria, taught that "the Logos is a creature called into being by God 'out of nonexistence.' As a creature, the Logos was subject to change and capable, at least in principle, of either virtue or vice, just as human beings were. Moreover, Arius taught, there was a 'time'—a 'when'—in which the Son/Logos did not yet exist."[6]

The council adopted a stance that refuted Arius's teaching, declaring that the Son is in essence eternal with God.

Mormons, while not necessarily supporting the Arian position, do mark this council as a turning point of the Church (see chapter 4, n. 3). Moreover, they not only support the concept of the Son being generated from nonexistence and thus a being separate in essence from the Father but go far beyond Arius to affirm a plurality of many gods, of which Heavenly Father, The Savior, and the Holy Ghost are but three.

The Father and the Son according to Mormon theology are separate persons whose bodies are limited to flesh and bones, and in that separateness the Father and the Son are as bodily distinct from each other and from the Holy Ghost as Abraham Lincoln was from Jefferson Davis.

Following Nicaea, the Western arm of the Church carefully defined the Trinity as one God in three distinct persons, all of one essence. The major difference between mainstream

Christianity and Mormonism revolves around the difficulty of understanding this concept. This difficulty has caused more controversy in the Church than any other doctrine. Indeed Joseph Smith noted that one God in three is a strange kind of God. The main reason for this problem is that we are trying to describe God in terms consistent with our own level of existence and compare His person with that of a mortal human being. Yet when we are contemplating a God who created the universe and all the galaxies and stars and microbes that exist independently, we are considering Someone who is so far above us in essence that we cannot comprehend His dimensions, let alone His composition.

As the Council of Nicaea decided, God is unchanging and uncaused. He is the absolute first cause of all that exists. He cannot be placed upon a shelf or closed up in a box. What He is made of or how He exists we cannot say. Yet based on how He has revealed himself through nature, life, and the Holy Scriptures, we with the council can affirm Him to be one God in whom there are three distinct persons united in shared essence.

It is this essence Christians witness to when they speak of God's presence indwelling through the Holy Spirit. Mormons also testify to the Holy Spirit's indwelling. However, there is a difference here in that to the Christian the Holy Spirit is a distinct person sharing the same essence of the other persons of the Trinity. Within the Spirit resides the fullness of the godhead (Father, Son, and Holy Spirit) through this shared essence. Col. 2:9-10 alludes to this: "In him [Christ] dwelleth all the fullness of the Godhead bodily. And ye are complete in him, which is the head of all principality and power" (KJV). The message here is twofold: First, in Christ all the fullness of the Godhead lives in bodily form through the shared essence. This fullness includes the Father, Son, and Holy Spirit. Second, this fullness indwelling Christ also indwells believers through the Holy Spirit's sharing in the Godhead's one essence (see John 17:20-23; 1 John 4:15; Eph. 3:16-19). When the mark of a Christian is defined as the indwelling fullness of the Godhead, this is not a linguistic or cultural connection but a relational one.

The Mormon identification of the Holy Ghost as a spirit (not a person) separate in essence from the Father and Son stands in stark contrast. The priesthood blessing of bestowing the Holy Ghost is a Mormon tradition. Mormon Elder Dallin H. Oaks, of the Quorum of the Twelve Apostles, speaking before the Salt Lake City General Conference in 1996, stated that the "comforter, which is otherwise referred to as the Holy Ghost, . . . dwells in us."[7] Yet the teaching of a separation in essence of the Holy Ghost from the other persons of the Trinity surfaces in Joseph Smith's words when he wrote: "The idea that the Father and the Son dwell in a man's heart is an old sectarian notion, and is false."[8] If the Holy Ghost doesn't share the same essence with the other persons of the Trinity, then there is no fullness of the Godhead to indwell believers. Thus by Mormonism's own definition a person faithful to LDS teaching cannot by biblical definition be called a Christian because the concept of the fullness of the Godhead does not correspond to what Mormons teach about the nature of God.

Joseph Smith, Brigham Young, and Bruce McConkie, whose collective discourses spanned more than a hundred years of Mormon thought, taught that the resurrection would find certain men elevated to the status of gods and others to the position of angels. These teachings have been the center of Mormon belief and striving from the very beginning. Becoming gods, while not having a relationship with the one and only God, remains the central focus of the male quest for achieving a worthy evaluation in the priesthood to this very day.

It is clear from the LDS definition and the testimony of President Hinckley that the Jesus Christ of Mormonism is not the same Jesus Christ of traditional Christianity or of biblical revelation.

Brian Woodford, who for 17 years was a member of the LDS Church, working his way up to a bishopric in Salt Lake City, found nothing being preached from a Mormon pulpit to lead to salvation in Jesus Christ. He quoted one Mormon woman as confessing that, "I don't come to church to hear about Jesus; I come to learn how to raise my children."[9]

The tragedy of Woodford's testimony is that the doing and activities of working one's way into salvation deprive the soul of a relationship of intimate and eternal friendship. Mormons feel that their religion is superior in every way. Yet there is a vacuum that begs to be filled with a personal assurance of salvation here in this life.

Woodford confessed that he found his way out of the Mormon maze when he did something he had never done before as a Mormon. He said that after asking the Holy Spirit for guidance, "I realized that I could not know Christ and be a Mormon."[10] Woodford's confession offers insight into the missing link in so many experiences. The Word of God emerging from the pages of a Bible has no life until the Holy Spirit speaks through the written page.

In variance to the office of knowledge, as perceived in the LDS picture of God, the missing link to completeness in a person's spiritual life is a relationship with God. It is the tree of life as opposed to the tree of knowledge. Joseph Smith opted for knowledge and not life. Mormonism seeks knowledge and avoids life. The purpose for human life is to experience a relationship with God rather than achieve independence through knowledge. The personal touch of a relationship with God is the missing link in an LDS experience.

A little tract by Melaine Layton of Wheeling, Illinois, records her journey out of Mormonism following a troubling internal conflict with her Mormon testimony. She relates what triggered her exodus, "As I read the Bible, I found so many things that contradicted Mormon teaching."[11]

Mormons are seeking a relationship but are misguided as to where to look for it. Their rules, tests, ordinances, rituals, and societies are designed to give them this missing dimension in their lives. Writing in USA Today, Grant Jerding noted that "most converts [to Mormonism] say they find a connection that was, until conversion, missing."[12] The missing element in most instances is a feeling of being cared for as an individual person. The family structure of the LDS ward* community provided what is missing in so many lives isolated from true caring fellowship.

This should alert Christians to the need that is widespread across our nation for relationship building within the community of faith. We Christians say we have a relationship with God but often fail in our relationships with one another. The Mormons claim relationships with one another but fail in their relationship with God. As a result, people are searching but are unable to find satisfying results in both directions at the same time. Men and women have a design inherited from creation that pants for relationship. We need caring, loving nurture in this physical life, but that is not enough. We also need a relationship with things that are eternal.

Mormon apostle Robert D. Hales, speaking before the 1996 General Conference of the LDS Church in Salt Lake City, reminded Mormons that eternity is just a big family reunion that can be achieved "through making and keeping the sacred covenants found in the temple ordinances."[13] The Mormon hope of relationship does not look forward to a personal friendship with God so much as it foresees a continuation of the earthly family who are sealed to them for eternity.

I remember the feeling of aloneness once felt by former LDS member Mike.** His strongest desire was for God to come and sit down across the table from him so that he could have some kind of personal encounter with Him. He felt betrayed because this never happened. So, in frustration, because he wanted that relationship so badly, he was ready to duke it out with God just to experience His closeness. "If You can't hug me, then slug me" was his attitude. Mormons want a God with whom they can sit down across the table and talk to like a friend. They want a divine companionship that is re-

---

*See "Glossary of LDS Words," page 87.
**Assumed name

al and alive here in this life. Yet that sense of intimate friendship is denied them, and they are left to work out their lives in the hope that they will be found worthy when all humankind is assembled before Joseph Smith, Jesus Christ, and Heavenly Father on the Mormon judgment day.

In 1979 BYU religion professor George Pace encouraged his students to pursue a personal relationship with The Savior. As a result of his teaching, Elder Bruce McConkie castigated Professor Pace publicly. Subsequently the professor made a public apology for teaching about a "wrong" relationship with The Savior. There are mixed feelings to this day about this subject among Mormons. The truth is that LDS doctrines deny the Mormon any personal friendship with God either in this life or the life to come.

The longing and desire are there. Mormons want to belong, to be accepted, and it is through this hunger that a Christian witness can gently open the blinded eyes to God's prevenient grace. It is God's desire that all respond to His calling and accept the atonement of Jesus' sacrifice at Calvary for the forgiveness of all their sins (see 2 Pet. 3:9).

Paul preached "that Christ died for our sins . . . that he was buried, that he was raised on the third day according to the Scriptures" (see 1 Cor. 15:1-4). This is the gospel message that Jesus brought to the earth. The Mormon gospel is labored with moving the Atonement off of the Cross and into the Garden of Gethsemane where it does not atone for all human sin but only for the sin of Adam. The Mormon gospel teaches faith, repentance, baptism, and the laying on of hands for the gift of the Holy Ghost but overlooks a relationship of grace in the progression of works. The critical issue here is that a witness needs to convey the personal relationship that Jesus died for his or her sins, personally, and not Adam's sin only—but the witness's sins!

We who profess to be Christians leave a vacuum in our community that often denies the human need for love and companionship with one another. As a result, professing Christians leave the church to join the fellowship of Mor-

mons or other relationship-promising cults. Yet in the LDS
religion a vacuum exists in which intimacy with Heavenly
Father and Jesus Christ is wanting; thus many are seeking this
sort of closeness elsewhere. The LDS structure substitutes
God's companionship for a relationship with the family for all
time and eternity. For some that seems to satisfy their longing, at least intellectually.

We can each learn from one another. We of the Christian
faith can revisit the Book of Acts and the Epistles and
Gospels to restore the intimate relationships of serving one
another, of community structure and *agape* love. We can build
this kind of *koinōnia* fellowship and practice it in our daily
lives. That will shut the back door, and as we develop the intimate relationship with God in His fullness through Jesus,
our Lord, we will open wide the front door.

# 10

# THE MORMON MIRACLE

WE HAD NOT BEEN IN OUR NEW HOME long when two young men dressed in black slacks, white shirts, and ties came to the door. Each was carrying what appeared to be a rather thick Bible bag. They were neat, friendly, and courteous. They were Mormon missionaries. I was amazed. Here we were in the very heart of conservative Mormonism—Provo, Utah, the intellectual pulse of the Mormon world, and yet the Mormon missionaries were hard at work seeking converts right in their own backyard.

From kindergarten through high school Mormon children are encouraged to plan on a mission. Their parents plan for it. Training prepares them mentally and psychologically for this, the eminent event in their religious career. When a young person enters high school, he or she is expected to attend seminary, which is a released-time class for learning about Mormonism. The ward provides seminary training in cooperation with school, off campus, during schooltime. Young people go on their missions following high school and before entering college. Their first commitment is to the church; then what's left of life can follow.

Regardless of where in the world a family lives, the sequence is the same. When a young person applies for a mission, the first step is to obtain a bishop's recommendation. Then the petition is passed on to the stake* president and finally the general authority, whose office is in Salt Lake City. All requests for missions are finally signed by the president of

*See "Glossary of LDS Words," page 87.

the church, who is the living prophet. The prospective missionary is then notified, and a slot is opened at the Missionary Training Center (MTC) in Provo, Utah, for preparation.

The church does not pay missionaries. Each missionary is responsible for paying his or her own way with the help of parents, extended family, and friends and by working and saving. When the means are secured, the student then enters the MTC.

There are two tracks in the training curriculum—one for two months for those who will learn a foreign language and another for four weeks for missionaries who go to English-speaking countries (including the United States). According to BYU authorities there are 2,000 seats for students at the MTC. There are approximately 55,000 missionaries in the field at all times in addition to their supervisors and administrative personnel.

With no graduation ceremony, a student finishes the last day of class work. On that very day his or her family members, if they are in the area, escort the new missionary to the International Airport at Salt Lake City. In the midst of a tremendous send-off, the young person and his or her fellow missionaries board a plane and fly to their mission destination. They wear dark suits and name tags identifying each man as "Elder so-and-so" and each woman as "Sister so-and-so." These young people move out to spread the Mormon gospel into the lives of people in nearly every country of the world. Mormon missionaries go out two by two; one disciplines the other. They are instructed never to be out of sight of each other at any time during their stay at the MTC or while on the mission field.

Eli,* a former LDS member, told me that the crowning achievement for parents is when they send their kids on a mission. "For my dad it was cheaper to support me in Argentina than it was at home anyway. We lived like kings

---

*Assumed name

down there on about $120 a month. You never have to pay rent; it's all taken care of by the church. Missionaries come and go, and the rent is all paid by the church."

During the two-year stay on a mission assignment each young person's family pays a monthly assessment to the LDS general authority. From that fund monthly checks are sent to the missionary's regional office where the financial needs of each person in the field are met according to the cost of living in the area where each serves. The idea is that each missionary receives according to his or her personal need. Every individual returning from a mission has a student slot available at BYU where he or she can gain a quality education. An opportunity to gain more knowledge is the reward for service.

I asked Eli, "When did you start preparing for your mission?"

"You start when you're a young kid," he replied. "You hope that they call you on a mission. A lot of time parents will start their kids collecting pennies when they're very young. When they are older, they save quarters and then dollars. Putting money away for a mission is a whole family savings program. 'You're going on a mission someday so you can serve the Lord,' they say to little boys. And they say to little girls, 'Keep yourself worthy so when you get a man someday, he can marry you in the temple.'*

". . . When you get older, you fill out all the papers, you get dental work done and all the rest. You send it all in to Salt Lake, and it's signed by the prophet in ink, in his hand.

"You really don't start getting prepared for the mission until you go to the MTC. Then it's seven days a week. Classes in the morning and afternoon. Teachers talk about the experiences they've had on their missions in morning devotionals. All the teachers at the MTC are returned missionaries. Usually BYU students.

---

*Young girls also go on missions, but the emphasis during their formative years is to prepare for temple marriage.

"You're supposed to be with your companion day and night, for 24 hours. We're told that's because the devil is doing everything he can to get at the missionaries. And another thing, you're not supposed to go into the water when on a mission except to baptize someone. They told us that Satan rules the waters and lots of elders have drowned. He's especially hard on missionaries they said.

"The routine on a mission is that you have one day that's called a P day. That means preparation day. It's when you do what you want. The other five days you go out two by two and knock on doors. On Sunday you try to bring your investigators, those who you've made curious, into church services.

"There are seven missionary discussions. You memorize each of those. Usually you give one discussion for one appointment with each of the non-Mormons you contact on the mission field. After you go through all seven discussions, you challenge them to be baptized. You ask them if they believe that Joseph Smith was a prophet of God. If they believe it, there is no reason why they can't be members of the church. You say, 'Are you willing to accept baptism?' They say either yes or no. If it's yes, you baptize them; if it's no, you go on to the next person.

"It doesn't seem to matter so much whether they acknowledge Jesus Christ as Lord, just as long as they believe that Joseph Smith was a prophet. That is significant, for when they believe in the office of Smith as a prophet, then whatever Smith has said about Jesus is truth to them. It doesn't seem to matter whether Smith's revelation of the gospel coincides with that found in the Bible just as long as converts believe that Smith was a prophet; his word is then final.

"One of the discussions is on repentance," Eli continued. "There are seven steps you have to go through in the repentance process. There's no such thing as instant forgiveness of sin. You have to go through these steps. You memorize them. You don't take them with you. Its all word for word—'Do you believe this?' We tell them that we have a president, apostles, and we have a living prophet. A lot of people come along who are interested in that. When we ask, 'If you knew there was a prophet today who could tell you how you're supposed to live your life, would you want to be a member of that?' 'Oh, yes, sure, if I knew,' they say, and that's when you convince them about Joseph Smith. If they bite on that, you can reel them in big time.

"I obeyed the rules because they told me to," said Eli. "Then what got me to question things was when a mission president taught me about the gray areas. He taught me that it wasn't bad to be in the gray areas some of the times by bending some of the rules. It preserves the peace in the district he said."

What are the results of all this LDS mission activity? The Latter-day Saints had their origin in the early 1800s, and by the turn of the century, there were approximately a quarter of a million Mormons isolated in the state of Utah. Today the LDS world population has exceeded 11 million. The reason for this rapid growth seems focused on the MTC and its impact on the world. According to Jeffery Sheler and Betsy Wagner, "Mormons already outnumber Presbyterians and Episcopalians combined."[1]

Ideally, there is a dedication, a lifetime purpose, and an eternal vision for each young person who grows up in the LDS faith. Underneath the surface there may be many cracks and fissures, but the ideal of Mormon training and practice is one of community and family focus that inspires dedication.

Why does the LDS movement sustain such rapid growth, even in areas that are hostile to their cult? Why are Evangelical Protestants unable to plant a church under similar circumstances in the heart of Morman Utah? And an even more relevant question is, What could Christendom learn from them? I think the answer lies in a lifeline that reaches from the cradle to the grave. It is a commitment to dedicated energy that encompasses everyone in the cultural web. It inspires pride as well as commitment in the hearts of the entire community.

Living in prime Mormon territory as a non-Mormon, my wife and I worked to establish an Evangelical church. We learned to focus upon our internal relations of loving one another and encouraging one another. We began to teach folks in our congregation how to have devotions and center their time around the family. We learned from the LDS community that in the neighborhoods, people cared for one another, helped one another, and organized safety and disaster preparedness teams, recreation activities, social events, and caring activities where they worked together. The wards looked out for everyone in the neighborhood, not just the LDS faithful. This gave them an excuse for being there when needed. They impressed others by their energy. Neighbors cared for and watched after children. Families were careful to train their children and inspire them to understand the history and tradition of the community.

Christianity can relearn the lessons of Acts as believers observe the structure and commitment of an LDS community. What they are doing is not a cult thing, but a Christian action that has long been absent in many Christian churches and neighborhoods. It is evident that such focus on the internal needs of the congregation inspires those within to reach out. The aura of clean living attracts others, and the result is the fastest growing cult on the face of the earth.

# 11

# DO DISTANT DRUMS THREATEN THE SECURITY OF THE VILLAGE?

WHY ARE MORMONS ANY MORE DANGEROUS to Christianity than Jehovah's Witnesses, Christian Science practitioners, or any number of other cults that make up the face of today's religious puzzle? Is it not true that Jesus taught that "the gates of hell shall not prevail against" His Church (Matt. 16:18, KJV)? Is it also not true that Satan has no power over Christ's Church?

However, take a lesson from history. Prior to the Islamic flood that swept over North Africa and much of the Middle East as well as parts of Europe, there was a thriving church in North Africa. At this early date Islam was virtually unknown anywhere outside of Arabia. Today the church in North Africa is impotent beneath the crushing weight of Islam. Much of the unrest in the Balkans is a direct result of the religious confrontation between Muslim and Christian peoples.

There are parallels between Islam and Mormonism that should enlist our attention. The means of conquest are different, yet the objective is the same—world domination. In the 10th century, Islam swept across the civilized world under the force of an idealism backed by military arms. Today 55,000 Mormon missionaries sweep across the civilized world with an idealist's zeal of sacrifice and hard work backed by an economic arsenal that is formidable. These parallels are both historical and contemporary. Today the primary focus of Mormon evangelism is directed to Christian population centers.

The majority of converts are professing Christians who see in Mormonism something they feel is missing in their traditional churches.

There are several factors that make Mormonism the most dangerous cult that has challenged Christianity since the Arian controversy of the third and fourth centuries.

1. The language of the Mormon missionary is essentially the same as the language of the traditional Christian.

2. Mormonism is one of the fastest growing religions on earth, and the growth momentum will carry many people along with the popular flow.

3. The forms of Mormonism are essentially the same forms as those exhibited in Christianity; thus it is difficult for many to see any differences.

4. The LDS religion is backed by solid financial resources and employs the most sophisticated state-of-the-art media technologies available. The more one is exposed to propaganda of this sort, the more one tends to believe that it is true. Mormonism is building an image in the guise of a Christian denomination that responds to the needs of family and country.

There are always rumors that the LDS community is falling apart. That is nothing more than wishful thinking. It is not happening. Many within the LDS community are dissatisfied with Mormonism for various reasons, but they are not exiting in droves. Rather, dissatisfaction is a characteristic of our society as a whole.

5. The LDS religion is led by businessmen who capitalize on their ability to sell a product. That product is a false religion based upon the imagination of a 19th-century charlatan named Joseph Smith.

6. LDS doctrine and structure parallels that of the end-time apostate church known as the beast of Revelation. The end-time false religion will be a church that will deceive. Jesus said that "false prophets will appear and perform great signs and miracles to deceive even the elect—if that were possible" (Matt. 24:24). Whether or not there is a parallel between Mormonism and the beast of Revelation will only be

realized by history, but the earmarks of the end-time religion are solidly implanted in LDS structure and theology.

Regardless of the eschatological potential of the LDS religion, it is a cult that drinks from the lifeblood of Christianity and siphons off many into its clutches every day. In analyzing our early definition of the cult (pp. 13-14), we can see the marks of Mormonism in each of the categories. It is clear that Mormonism is not a Christian religion and that it is definitely a product of the cult.

1. The person and authority of God is diminished.

In Mormonism God is reduced to a mortal creature who has attained his status as CEO of this world through working his way from mortality to immortality and Celestial godhood. Jesus Christ is his procreated child who attained godhood through good works in much the same way that all faithful Mormon men have the potential of doing.

2. The authority and accuracy of Scripture is questioned to allow for new revelation that supplants biblical precepts.

According to the *Book of Mormon,* "After the book [Bible] hath gone forth through the hands of the great and abominable church, that there are many plain and precious things taken away from the book, which is the book of the Lamb of God."[1] As a result of his denial of the accuracy of Scripture, Smith was able to add new books to his version of the canon that supplanted Bible truths with his own ideas and theology.

3. The pregrace condition of humankind is not that of being hopelessly lost.

This idea is found in the Mormon story telling why Adam came to earth and how the Fall was really a thrilling event opening the way for humankind to enjoy the opportunity of attaining godhood. In this story we have no lost world but rather a world on its way to fulfilling the plan and purpose of God. It is this very story that Satan told Eve in the garden that lured her to eat of the forbidden fruit. The fate that awaited Adam and Eve for their disobedience is the same fate that awaits the Mormon man who wishes to outdistance God in his self-preserving quest to become a god in the exaltation.

4. Jesus Christ is not the only way to God.

The way to God is, for the Mormon, a very confusing path. Jesus is one of the ways, Joseph Smith another, and those of the Mormon priesthood another.

5. Humankind is not dependent entirely upon Christ's atonement but can achieve some form of salvation through personal merit.

Mormons teach that the atonement of Jesus is not sufficient to bring one into salvation. Instead, the worthy Mormon has to work for a status in eternity, and the only sacrifice sufficient to cleanse away personal sin is the shedding of the Mormon's own blood.

In all five cases Mormonism comes up short of the measuring rod that determines Christianity. When dealing with Mormons, it is difficult to keep focused on the issues that measure truth. The LDS missionary and other witnesses are taught to move the discussion away from things that question the authority of their doctrines and beliefs. When a question gets Mormon missionaries in too deep, they will ask for time to consult with someone else for an answer. When there is no satisfactory answer, the response will usually be, "We are not permitted to know this in this dispensation, but it will all be revealed by Heavenly Father in his time."

It will be difficult to get a Mormon to stick to the main issues, but that will be necessary if there is to be any resolution or conviction. The two issues that are most critical are the nature of God and the means of revelation. Most other things that Mormons want to talk about, or that many Christians get caught up in (such as polygamy, Black priests, etc.) are of little importance until after the issue of God is settled. If a person does not know what God is like, it is impossible for him or her to worship the one true God. If the means of revelation is not settled, false notions about God will surface and the nature of God will remain confused.

# Appendix 1
# COMPARING LDS DISTINCTIVES WITH CHRISTIAN DISTINCTIVES

The highest percentage of all those who convert into Mormonism are professing Christians. Many believe that Mormonism is just another Christian denomination, so in their minds there is little difference between joining the Mormon church or a Presbyterian church or some other denomination.

When the beliefs of Mormonism are compared with the words of the Bible, there is often some similarity, but on issues important to salvation the two are far apart.

## The Person of God

### Mormon

LDS faith teaches the following:

There are multiple gods.

God's majesty is intelligence not holiness.

The Mormon gods were once mortal men who achieved their godhood through merit.

All gods have multiple wives.

Each wife of the gods procreates numerous spirit children and continues to give birth for all eternity.

### Christian

"Before me no god was formed, nor will there be one after me. I, even I, am the LORD, and apart from me there is no savior" (Isa. 43:10-11).

"Hear, O Israel: The LORD our God, the LORD is one" (Deut. 6:4).

"In the beginning was the Word, and the Word was with God, and the Word was God. He was with God in the beginning. Through him all things

Human men living today, if worthy, can become gods in the afterlife.

were made; without him nothing was made that has been made. . . . The Word became flesh and made his dwelling among us" (John 1:1-3, 14).

## Creation

### Mormon

In the temple ceremony temple worthies are told that when God came to bring the world into being, He was confronted with "matter unorganized" and from that he formed the worlds. Humankind itself was never actually created—but humankind's intelligence has existed coeternally with God for eternity without origin.

Numerous personages who were found to be good in the preexistence were made rulers and are called the noble and great ones.

### Christian

"In the beginning God created the heavens and the earth" (Gen. 1:1).

"For he spoke, and it came to be; he commanded, and it stood firm" (Ps. 33:9).

"He is the image of the invisible God, the firstborn over all creation. For by him all things were created: things in heaven and on earth, visible and invisible, whether thrones or powers or rulers or authorities; all things were created by him and for him. He is before all things, and in him all things hold together. And he is the head of the body, the church; he is the beginning and the firstborn from among the dead, so that in everything he might have the supremacy. For God was pleased to have all his fullness dwell in him, and through him to reconcile to himself all things, whether things on earth or things in heaven, by making peace through his blood, shed on the cross" (Col. 1:15-20).

# Justification by Faith and Repentance

## Mormon

Many portions of the Bible are not reliable because they do not agree with that which was revealed to the LDS prophets.

Adam was sent to earth to fall from his immortal state so that he could provide a way for spirit babies to come to earth as mortals with the potential of working their way into being gods themselves. Thus there was no Fall, but rejoicing in the fulfillment of this great and noble accomplishment.

In LDS teaching humankind is not fallen, but all will be resurrected into immortality.

The only salvation is through the LDS gospel, the LDS priesthood, and the LDS sealing ceremonies participated in through the LDS temple. The LDS teaching claims that only through gospel obedience in the restoration brought about by Joseph Smith and only through the LDS Church is salvation available to any mortal human being.

## Christian

"It is by grace you have been saved. And God raised us up with Christ and seated us with him in the heavenly realms in Christ Jesus, in order that in the coming ages he might show the incomparable riches of his grace, expressed in his kindness to us in Christ Jesus. For it is by grace you have been saved, through faith—and this not from yourselves, it is the gift of God—not by works, so that no one can boast" (Eph. 2:5-9).

# Atonement

## Mormon

Mormonism teaches that the atonement that brings immortality (restoring mortality with immortality) was brought about in the Garden of Gethsemane when Jesus shed His blood (sweat drops of blood) in prayer. They deny the Cross, for it is an involuntary execution, thus inappropriate to serve as a basis for atonement. However, atonement that leads to eternal life (ascendancy into the Celestial kingdom) is dependent upon our own works and sacrifice.

The LDS faith concludes that there are certain sins of such magnitude that the atonement of Christ is not effective. The law of God, they claim, concludes that to be forgiven of such sins the individual seeking forgiveness must have his or her own blood shed to gain atonement.

The State of Utah, which is largely populated by LDS adherents, allows for a firing squad to execute prisoners sentenced to death by the state. Such an execution would cause the shedding of blood.

## Christian

In Old Testament theology atonement is a covering—thus a covering of sin to allow sinful humans into the presence of God. The act of atonement that Christ performed on the Cross at Calvary was the shedding of innocent blood that becomes our only covering to wash away the stain of sin from our lives. (Sin is rebellion that causes separation from God. As long as sin reigns in our lives, we are unable to be restored to a relationship with God.) When our sin is covered by Jesus' blood, the relationship is restored.

"The blood of Jesus Christ his Son cleanseth us from all sin" (1 John 1:7, KJV).

"Therefore as by the offence of one judgment came upon all men to condemnation; even so by the righteousness of one the free gift came upon all men unto justification of life. . . . That as sin hath reigned unto death, even so might grace reign through righteousness unto eternal life by Jesus Christ our Lord" (Rom. 5:18, 21, KJV).

"And by that will, we have been made holy through the sacrifice of the body of Jesus Christ once for all" (Heb. 10:10).

"For God was pleased to have all his fullness dwell in him, and through him to reconcile to himself all things, whether things on earth or things in heaven, by making peace through his blood, shed on the cross" (Col. 1:19-20).

## Condition of Humankind

### Mormon

LDS teaching concludes that those who believe in traditional Christian teachings are damned.

The penalty for refusing to accept the LDS gospel, celestial marriage, or any other LDS covenant is damnation.

Assignment to the Terrestrial and Telestial kingdoms of immortality is dependent upon one's works here upon earth. The Telestial kingdom will be the place where most murderers and others who are bad are destined to spend eternity, yet it will be better than what earth is like in this life.

### Christian

"For God so loved the world that he gave his one and only Son, that whoever believes in him shall not perish but have eternal life. For God did not send his Son into the world to condemn the world, but to save the world through him. Whoever believes in him is not condemned, but whoever does not believe stands condemned already because he has not believed in the name of God's one and only Son" (John 3:16-18).

# Definition of Christianity

## Mormon

Christianity has its beginning in Adam. It includes all of the saints during all of the ages of humankind's existence who have accepted the Mormon gospel. That gospel was renewed by Jesus Christ when He came to earth. Jesus Christ was first born in the preexistence as a spirit child of Heavenly Father and one of his wives. Then He attained His mortal birth when born of Mary who was made pregnant by Heavenly Father's physical presence. Then the gospel was lost to the earth following the death of the last apostle. It was not until Joseph Smith restored this gospel to the earth that it was again possible for men and women to follow the true gospel.

**For further study into these doctrines, please consult the bibliography for publications by the following authors:**
    Bruce McConkie
    Orson Pratt
    Joseph Smith
    Joseph Fielding Smith
    James A. Talmage

## Christian

"The disciples were called Christians first at Antioch" (Acts 11:26).

"For in Christ all the fullness of the Deity lives in bodily form, and you have been given fullness in Christ, who is the head over every power and authority" (Col. 2:9-10).

# Appendix 2
## OTHER GROUPS

In addition to the Utah-based LDS there is the Missouri-based Reorganized Church of Jesus Christ of Latter-day Saints (RLDS). The RLDS rejected Brigham Young as the leader following Smith's Death. They contended that Smith designated his son to succeed him as president. After a time of confusion, Joseph Smith, the son of the founder, was chosen president of the RLDS at Amboy, Illinois, in 1860. All presidents of the RLDS have been descendants of the founder. Headquarters for this group are located in Independence, Missouri.

Another group, also having its headquarters in Missouri, is the Church of Christ "Temple Lot." According to Frank Mead, followers of this branch believe "that the Lord himself will designate the time of building [the temple], and that while the men of the church cannot do this until the appointed time, they nevertheless believe that they have a sacred obligation to hold and keep this land [plots of land in Independence, Mo.] free, 'that when the time of building does come, it can be accomplished as the Lord sees fit'"[1]

A third branch is the Church of Jesus Christ. According to Mead, "the founders of this body were at one time members of a Mormon body led by Sidney Rigdon, in Pennsylvania. Rigdon and his followers refused to join the western march under Brigham Young, denouncing Young's teaching of polygamy, the plurality of gods, and baptism for the dead."[2] Their headquarters is in Mongahala, Pennsylvania.

A fourth group, known as the Church of Jesus Christ of Latter-day Saints (Strangites), takes its name after its founder James J. Strang, who claimed to be the only legal successor to church leadership with written credentials from Joseph Smith. Mead writes that this group, "organized at Burlington, Wisconsin, in 1844, . . . denies the virgin birth theory, holds that Adam fell by a law of natural consequences rather than in the breaking of a divine law, and that the corruption thus caused could be removed only by the resurrection of Christ. They deny the Trinity and the plurality of gods, celebrate Saturday as the Sabbath day, and believe that baptism is essential for salvation."[3]

Other churches would include the Perfected Church of Jesus Christ the Immaculate Latter-day Saints, the Church of the First Born of the Fullness of Times, and many more, all of whom have small memberships. A sizeable number of Fundamentalist bodies, estimated by some authorities to number around 40,000, continue to actively practice polygamy in parts of Utah, Arizona, and Nevada. The most notable of these enclaves of polygamy are located in Colorado City, Arizona, and in Hildale, Utah.

# GLOSSARY OF LDS WORDS*

**Adam.** Led the righteous angels in the victorious battle that resulted in casting Lucifer and his rebels out of the preexistence. He is the archangel Michael. Adam was placed on earth as an immortal (no blood) and could not have children. Adam had to choose between disobeying God by eating of the fruit of the tree of the knowledge of good and evil and disobeying God by not having children, which would have been the result had he not eaten of the fruit that made him mortal. Adam wisely chose the sin that made it possible for all people to inherit eternal life. The result is that Adam fell up and is revered in Mormon doctrine as second only to Christ in power and intelligence.

**Aaronic Priesthood.** Joseph Smith and Oliver Cowdery were conferred the Aaronic Priesthood, May 15, 1829, by John the Baptist. This priesthood is for males 12 years and older.

**Baptism.** The only recognized baptism must be performed by an authorized member of the priesthood, by immersion of those 8 years old or older.

**Baptism for the dead.** Many people have not been given the opportunity to be baptized in their own lifetime because of the accident of birth. To provide the opportunity to all whom God has overlooked, the LDS Church performs such sacraments in its temples by proxy for the dead. In order to perform these rituals the names must be presented, and that is one reason Mormons have an extensive preoccupation with genealogy.

**Bishop.** The presiding ward officer.

**Branch.** A developing ward.

---

*With some exception, the wording and contents of this glossary are from the pamphlet *A Lexicon of LDS Terminology*, assembled by the First Presbyterian Church, Salt Lake City, and are used by permission.

**Creation.** A re-forming of eternally existent matter, energy, and spirit. There is no actual creation, the making of something from nothing.

**Elder.** Ordained men at least 18 years of age. Includes most active male LDS Church members.

**General authority.** Leaders holding the highest authority in the church.

**Gentile.** Any person who is not a Mormon.

**God.** There are many gods. Gods have physical bodies. Each man has the potential of becoming a god of his own world. Our planet is governed by Heavenly Father (Elohim). There are three separate gods who have jurisdiction here; they are Heavenly Father, Jesus Christ—The Savior, and the Holy Ghost.

**Gospel.** Through obedience to the gospel (baptism, tithing, Celestial marriage, temple work, priesthood, and various other rituals) only the male has the potential to achieve godhood. The female is dependent upon her husband (either by temple marriage in this life or by proxy marriage after she has died) to call her from the grave in order to be resurrected into the Celestial kingdom. All other females will be resurrected into one of the inferior kingdoms where they will spend eternity as servants to those of higher standing.

**Grace.** Grace is conferred on those who conform to the standards of personal righteousness.

**Hell.** This is a temporary place of punishment where wicked spirits go until released into the Telestial kingdom. Those who have committed the unpardonable sin go into banishment or outer darkness with Lucifer and his fallen angels for everlasting torment.

**Holy Ghost.** A god, separate from Heavenly Father and Jesus, who is Spirit rather than flesh and bones and does indwell the faithful Mormon.

**Lucifer.** Younger brother of Jesus who led a rebellion against Heavenly Father.

**Marriage.** Marriage outside of the temple is only for this life. Marriage sealed in the temple is for eternity. A Mormon is baptized to enter the gate into the Celestial kingdom. The Celestial marriage ceremony is to enter the gate into exaltation in the Celestial kingdom.

**Melchizedek Priesthood.** Peter, James, and John restored the ancient Melchizedek Priesthood in June of 1829 upon Joseph Smith and Oliver Cowdery.

**Paradise.** Where worthy Latter-day Saints go immediately following death to await the judgment when they will be invited into the Celestial kingdom.

**Preexistence.** In a time of preexistence Heavenly Father, along with his many wives, procreate spirit children. For the most part spirit children are incapable of progression until they inhabit human bodies. Thus in the preexistence each human was first born, and when a human baby is born on earth, one of Heavenly Father's spirit children inhabits the human body. Although it is not fully explained in LDS literature, there were some worthies who merited godhood in the preexistence. Included in this number was Jesus Christ.

**Priesthood.** The only authority to perform church ordinances recognized by the LDS Church is that of the priesthood as restored to Joseph Smith. Priesthood offices are reserved to male members only. There is no paid clergy in the LDS religion.

**Scriptures.** Mormon scriptures include the King James Version of the Bible "in so far as it is correctly translated," the *Book of Mormon, The Doctrine and Covenants,* and *The Pearl of Great Price.*

**Spirit Prison.** The place where all non-LDS people go immediately following death. LDS missionaries come from paradise and preach the gospel that they may have an opportunity to advance into one of the lesser kingdoms of the Mormon heaven.

**Stake.** The administrative office that presides over a number of wards.

**Temple.** Sanctuaries where sacred ordinances, rites, and ceremonies are performed. Only temple-worthy Mormons are permitted entrance.

**Ward.** A single Mormon congregation, generally not more than 400 members.

# NOTES

**Introduction**

1. "Deseret" is a word in reformed Egyptian (a language known only by Joseph Smith) from the *Book of Mormon* meaning "honeybee." It was the original name given to the western territory into which the early Latter-day Saints migrated.

2. Katy Kelly, "Mormons on Mission to Grow," *USA Today*, 21 October 1997, 2D.

3. David Van Biema, "Kingdom Come," *Time*, 4 August 1997, 54.

4. Associated Press, "LDS Urged to Be Political," *(Provo, Utah) Daily Herald*, 3 February 1998, A2.

**Chapter 1**

1. Joseph Fielding Smith, *Teachings of the Prophet Joseph Smith* (Salt Lake City: Deseret Book Company, 1976), 345.

2. Brigham Young, *Journal of Discourses*, 26 vols. (Los Angeles: Gartner Printing and Litho Company, 1956), 1:123.

3. This includes both those who are alive contemporary with him, as well as those who, after death, are called by him through an endowment and temple marriage with the dead.

4. James A. Talmage, *A Study of the Articles of Faith* (Salt Lake City: Church of Jesus Christ of Latter-day Saints, 1950), 430.

5. Orson Pratt, ed., *The Seer* 1, no. 3 (March 1853): 158.

6. M. Russell Ballard, *Our Search for Happiness* (Salt Lake City: Deseret Book Company, 1993), 9.

**Chapter 2**

1. David Breese, *Know the Marks of Cults* (Wheaton, Ill.: Victor Books, 1988), 13.

2. Joseph Smith, *The Pearl of Great Price*, in *The Doctrine and Covenants of the Church of Jesus Christ of Latter-day Saints* [and] *The Pearl of Great Price* (Salt Lake City: Church of Jesus Christ of Latter-day Saints, 1982), History 1:15-19. Footnote g ascribes the person of his son to be "Jesus Christ, Divine Sonship."

3. LDS teaching supposes that an apostasy of belief followed the death of the last apostle. From that time onward until Joseph Smith stumbled upon the Father and Son in the woods near his New York home, the Church was in total error. This vision in the woods heralded the restoration of the

gospel through the prophet Joseph Smith. Subsequent to that event Christ restored His priesthood and through Smith reorganized His church.

4. Faun M. Brodie, *No Man Knows My History: The Life of Joseph Smith* (New York: Alfred A. Knopf, 1945), 74.

## Chapter 3

1. Smith, *Teachings,* 370.

2. Ibid., 345-46.

3. Bruce R. McConkie, *Mormon Doctrine,* 2d. ed. (Salt Lake City: Publishers Press, 1986), 576-77.

4. Smith, *Teachings,* 371.

5. William L. Holladay, ed., *A Concise Hebrew and Aramaic Lexicon of the Old Testament* (Grand Rapids: William B. Eerdmans Publishing Company, 1988), 329.

6. McConkie, *Mormon Doctrine,* 322-23.

7. James E. Ford, "What Mormons Believe," *Newsweek,* 1 September 1980, 68.

## Chapter 4

1. Joseph Smith, *Book of Mormon* (Salt Lake City: Church of Jesus Christ of Latter-day Saints, 1986), 1 Nephi 13:18-29.

2. Ballard, *Our Search for Happiness,* 27, 42.

3. LDS teaching contends that during the reign of Emperor Constantine and particularly during the Council at Nicaea, in Bithynia, in June A.D. 325, a compromise was reached between the Roman government and the Church that made the Church more secular than spiritual, with the true gospel being lost.

4. McConkie, *Mormon Doctrine,* 99.

5. Joseph B. Wirthlin, "Christians in Belief and Action," *Ensign,* November 1996, 70-71.

6. *Unger's New Bible Dictionary,* s.v. "Heart."

7. Judy Robertson, *No Regrets: How I Found My Way out of Mormonism* (Indianapolis: Light and Life Communications, 1997), 129.

## Chapter 5

1. Smith, *Doctrine and Covenants,* in *The Doctrine and Covenants* [and] *The Pearl of Great Price,* 93:29.

2. McConkie, *Mormon Doctrine,* 589.

3. Smith, *Pearl of Great Price,* Abraham 3:22-28.

4. Smith, *Doctrine and Covenants,* 93:21-23.

5. Russell M. Nelson, "The Atonement," *Ensign,* November 1996, 33.

6. Young, *Journal of Discourses,* 3:247.

**Chapter 6**

1. McConkie, Mormon Doctrine, 92.
2. Ibid., 669-70.

**Chapter 7**

1. GaWaNi Pony Boy, *Horse, Follow Closely: Native American Horse-manship* (Irvine, Calif.: Bow Tie Press, 2001), 45.
2. Ibid., 37.
3. Mary Pipher, Ph.D., *Reviving Ophelia: Saving the Selves of Adolescent Girls* (New York: Ballantine Books, 1994), 190.

**Chapter 8**

1. The *Book of Mormon* describes a thriving civilization upon the American continent prior to the discovery of the Western world by Christopher Columbus. LDS scholars label this area Mesoamerica and attempt to locate the lands of Bountiful, Zarahemla, Nephi, and Desolation geographically. These are four geographical locations identified in the *Book of Mormon*.

**Chapter 9**

1. Hatch to Conlon, 24 August 1998.
2. Thomas S. Monson, *The Search for Jesus* (Salt Lake City: Deseret Book Company, 1990), 10.
3. Paul Hedengren, "Review of *Are Mormons Christian?* and *Offenders for a Word,*" *BYU Studies* 33, no. 3 (1993): 636.
4. R. Philip Roberts, "Thank You, Mr. President," *The Evangel,* January/February 1999, 8, quoting Gordon Hinckley, *Church News,* 20 June 1998, 7.
5. Williston Walker, et al., *A History of the Christian Church,* 4th ed. (New York: Charles Scribner's Sons, 1985), 81.
6. Ibid., 132.
7. Dallin H. Oaks, "Always Have His Spirit," *Ensign,* November 1996, 59.
8. Smith, *Doctrine and Covenants,* 130:3.
9. Woodford, "I Did Something," 3.
10. Ibid.
11. Melaine N. Layton, *Mormonism* (Wheeling, Ill.: Melaine Layton, 1975).
12. Grant Jerding, "Mormons on Mission to Grow," *USA Today,* 21 October 1997, 1.
13. Robert D. Hales, "The Eternal Family," *Ensign,* November 1996, 65.

**Chapter 10**

1. Jeffery L. Sheler and Betsy Wagner, "Latter Day Struggles," *U.S. News and World Report,* 28 September 1992, 73.

**Chapter 11**
   1. Smith, *Book of Mormon*, 1 Nephi 13:18-29.

**Appendix 2**
   1. Frank S. Mead, *Handbook of Denominations in the United States*, 5th ed. (Nashville: Abingdon Press, 1970), 82. Used by permission.
   2. Ibid., 82-83.
   3. Ibid., 83.

# BIBLIOGRAPHY

Baker, Don, and Emery Nester. *Depression, Finding Hope and Meaning in Life's Darkest Shadow*. Portland, Oreg.: Multnomah Press, 1977.

Ballard, M. Russell. *Our Search for Happiness*. Salt Lake City: Deseret Book Company, 1993.

Beattie, Melody. *Codependents' Guide to the Twelve Steps*. New York: Prentice Hall Press, 1990.

Brodie, Fawn M. *No Man Knows My History: The Life of Joseph Smith*. 2d ed. New York: Alfred A. Knopf, 1995.

Brown, S. Kent, Donald Q. Cannon, and Richard H. Jackson, eds. *Historical Atlas of Mormonism*. New York: Simon and Schuster, 1993.

Carter, Les, and Frank Minirth. *The Anger Workbook*. Nashville: Thomas Nelson Publishers, 1993.

Friends in Recovery. *The Twelve Steps: A Spiritual Journey*. Rev. ed. San Diego: RPI Publishing, 1994.

Friends in Recovery. *The Twelve Steps for Christians*. Julian, Cal.: RPI Publishing, 1994.

Geer, Thelma. *Mormonism, Mama, and Me*. Chicago: Moody Press, 1986.

Gorski, Terence T., and Merlene Miller. *Staying Sober: A Guide for Relapse Prevention*. Independence, Mo.: Herald House/Independence Press, 1986.

Hemfelt, Robert, Frank Minirth, and Paul Meier. *Love Is a Choice: Recovery for Codependent Relationships*. Nashville: Thomas Nelson Publishers, 1989.

Hart, Archibald D. *Unlocking the Mystery of Your Emotions*. Dallas: Word Publishers, 1989.

Hinckley, Gordon. "Believing in Christ." *LDS Church News*, 2 January 1999.

Holladay, William L., ed. *A Concise Hebrew and Aramaic Lexicon of the Old Testament*. Grand Rapids: William B. Eerdmans Publishing Company, 1988.

*I Need a Friend: A Friendshipping Guide for Members of the Church*. Salt Lake City: Church of Jesus Christ of Latter-day Saints, 1977.

Layton, Melaine N. *Mormonism*. Wheeling, Ill.: Melaine Layton, 1975.

McConkie, Bruce R. *Mormon Doctrine*. 2d ed. Salt Lake City: Publishers Press, 1986.

McKeever, Bill. *Answering Mormons' Questions*. Minneapolis: Bethany House Publishers, 1991.

Minirth, Frank B. and Paul D. Meier. *Happiness Is a Choice*. Grand Rapids: Baker Book House, 1978.

Monson, Thomas S. *The Search for Jesus*. Salt Lake City: Deseret Book Company, 1990.

Pipher, Mary. *Reviving Ophelia: Saving the Selves of Adolescent Girls*. New York: Ballantine Books, 1994.

Pratt, Orson. *The Seer*. Washington City, D.C., edited and published by Orson Pratt, Vol 1, Number 3, March 1853.

Robertson, Judy. *No Regrets: How I Found My Way out of Mormonism*. Indianapolis: Light and Life Communications, 1997.

Ross, Ron. *When I Grow Up I Want to Be an Adult*. San Diego: Recovery Publications, 1990.

Seamonds, David. *Healing for Damaged Emotions*. Wheaton, Ill.: Scripture Press, 1981.

Smalley, Gary and John Trent. *Love Is a Decision*. Dallas: Word Publishing, 1989.

Smith, John L. *Witnessing Effectively to Mormons*. Marlow, Okla.: Utah Missions, 1975.

Smith, Joseph. *Book of Mormon*. Salt Lake City: Church of Jesus Christ of Latter-day Saints, 1986.

————. *The Doctrine and Covenants* [and] *The Pearl of Great Price*. Salt Lake City: Church of Jesus Christ of Latter-day Saints, 1982.

Smith, Joseph Fielding. *Teachings of the Prophet Joseph Smith*. Salt Lake City: Deseret Book Company, 1976.

Spencer, James R. *Have You Witnessed to a Mormon Lately*. Tarrytown, N.Y.: Chosen Books, 1987.

Talmage, James A. *A Study of the Articles of Faith*. Salt Lake City: Church of Jesus Christ of Latter-day Saints, 1950.

Welch, John W., ed. *Reexploring the Book of Mormon*. Salt Lake City: Deseret Book Company, 1992.

Widtoe, John Andreas. *Discourses of Brigham Young: Second President of the Church of Jesus Christ of Latter-day Saints*. Salt Lake City: Deseret Book Company, 1954.

Young, Brigham. *Journal of Discourses*. 26 vols. Los Angeles: Gartner Printing and Litho Company, 1956.